SHRIMP

By Jay Harlow

Photography by
Victor Budnik

Food Styling by
Karen Hazarian

CHRONICLE BOOKS • SAN FRANCISCO

Library of Congress Cataloging-in-Publication Data

Harlow, Jay, 1953–
    Shrimp / by Jay Harlow ; photography by Victor Budnik ; food
styling by Karen Hazarian.
        p.   cm.
    Bibliography: p.
    Includes index.
    ISBN 0-87701-662-3. — ISBN 0-87701-658-5 (pbk.)
    1. Cookery (Shrimp) I. Budnik, Victor. II. Hazarian, Karen.
III. Title.
TX754.S58H37 1989
641.6'95 — dc20   89-17261
                                                          CIP

Editing: Elaine Ratner and Pat Tompkins
Illustration: Susan Mattmann
Typography: Classic Typography, Ukiah, CA
Design: Schuettge & Carleton, Berkeley, CA
Produced by Astolat Productions, Berkeley, CA
Printed in Japan.

Distributed in Canada by Raincoast Books
112 East 3rd Avenue
Vancouver, B.C., V5T 1C8

10 9 8 7 6 5 4 3 2 1

Chronicle Books
275 Fifth Street
San Francisco, California 94103

Acknowledgments

Thanks to the following people and organizations for their assistance with this book:

Dick Schuettge, a first-rate designer, and the person who originally urged me to do this book.

Victor Budnik and Karen Hazarian, for making the recipes look more elegant and appetizing than I could have imagined.

Stan Shoptaugh of Classic Typography, Ukiah, CA, for patiently bearing with us through several design revisions.

At Chronicle Books, publisher Jack Jensen, David Barich, Bill LeBlond, and Mary Ann Gilderbloom, for their enthusiastic support of this book from the start. Pat Tompkins, for her sharp editorial eye.

Susan Mattmann, for her excellent illustrations and unwavering friendship.

Gina Farruggio, for help in developing and testing the recipes.

Annieglass Studios for their beautiful plates.

Janie Celeste Hewson for her support.

Special thanks are due to Holly Adrian and Shelly Tolman of Ocean Garden Products, San Diego, for technical information and help with photography; William Feltch of New England Shrimp Company, Ayer, MA, for generously sharing his time and expertise; Bob Rosenberry, editor and publisher of Aquaculture Digest, San Diego, for reviewing the aquaculture section and helping me better understand shrimp farming technology; and Dustin Chivers, Department of Invertebrate Zoology, California Academy of Sciences, who has helped me for years with questions on all sorts of crustaceans.

My thanks also to Paul Johnson, Joan Steele, and all the staff of Monterey Fish Company in Berkeley and San Francisco; William Dooms and Sol Barreto, Erin Sales International, Oakland; Doug Gutterman, The Fresh Prawn Company, South San Francisco; Dale Sims, Gulfwater Seafoods, San Francisco; Jeff Watkins, H&N Fish Company, San Francisco.

And finally, to Elaine Ratner, my editor and partner. Her name really belongs on the title page, as this book has been a joint effort from its conception. Whether tasting recipes or editing them, she has managed to keep the project on track and on schedule. I would think her the best possible editor a writer could have even if she weren't my wife.

Contents

Introduction

As I got into writing this book about shrimp, I found myself on a delightful trip back through my entire cooking career.

In my very first restaurant cooking job, fresh out of college, I learned to sauté a handful of jumbo shrimp, arrange them on a plate just so, and deglaze the pan with wine and lemon juice to make a simple sauce. A few years later, after a side trip into the wine business and a year of restaurant school, I found myself in an Italian restaurant kitchen. There we sautéed large shrimp "scampi-style," in a garlicky, peppery butter sauce. After a while I moved to the Hayes Street Grill in San Francisco, where we cooks jumped at every chance to get plump, roe-laden spot prawns from Santa Barbara, which we skewered and grilled over a charcoal fire.

Over the years travel added new experiences. From Bangkok I brought back memories of fiery shrimp curries, a barely cured shrimp ceviche bathed in coconut milk, and enormous river prawns stuffed with seasoned pork and grilled in the shell. Venice will always mean to me a creamy, pink and white risotto of mixed shellfish from the nearby Adriatic. I think often of the baked stuffed shrimp in a waterfront restaurant in New Bedford, Massachusetts, and a salad of cold cooked prawns from the North Atlantic joyfully devoured in a pub in Devonshire, England. And New Orleans! Shrimp Rémoulade, shrimp in gumbo and jambalaya, eggplant stuffed with shrimp . . .

Now, I don't claim that every memorable meal I have had included shrimp. But I am continually impressed by the worldwide popularity and culinary versatility of these cosmopolitan shellfish. The recipes in this book are a collection of my personal favorites. Some are familiar classics, some improvisations on traditional themes, some total inventions.

Jay Harlow
Berkeley, California

Shrimp Basics

A Large and Varied Family

Shrimp are among the most widely available and most widely used of seafoods. They are found from the equator to the polar seas, in open oceans, bays, estuaries, and even fresh water. More than 300 species of shrimp are fished worldwide for human consumption.

To bring some order to all this diversity, biologists classify shrimp into a complicated hierarchy of orders, superfamilies, families, and subfamilies, each of which may contain many species. In this book, I will focus on two main categories—warm-water (*penaeid*) species and cold-water (*caridean*) species—plus a few miscellaneous species.

"Shrimp" vs. "Prawns"

First, some terminology. In my travels and in talking to cooks from around the country, I have found some confusion over the names *shrimp* and *prawns*. Either term is likely to show up on menus, in magazines and cookbooks, and even at the fish counter. What's the difference between a shrimp and a prawn? The answer depends in part on where you live.

In the eastern United States, shrimp is the common name for all types and sizes, with some regional variations. In the Northeast, where I grew up (and where the local shrimp are on the small side), *shrimp* was a perjorative term for someone small and insignificant, a synonym for *runt*. Comedian George Carlin could always get a laugh from an audience of New Yorkers by simply referring to "jumbo shrimp." But I suspect the joke fell flat in the South, where all sizes from tiny to jumbo are known as shrimp.

On the West Coast, large shrimp (generally the warm-water types discussed in the next section) are mostly known as prawns, and the name shrimp is reserved for the small cooked and peeled variety. This can create some confusion, especially when easterners are talking to westerners. I once gave a friend a recipe for a pasta dish with shrimp, by which I meant peeled raw shrimp. The instructions said to sauté the shrimp until they turn white. My friend called later to say she couldn't understand why the shrimp never changed to white—they stayed pink. When I realized she had used cooked and peeled shrimp and explained I meant raw, she said, "Oh, you mean I was supposed to use prawns!"

The British call all shrimplike creatures *prawns* (except for some small northern types). That name persists in most British Commonwealth nations, including India, Hong Kong, Australia, and South Africa.

The United Nations Food and Agriculture Organization (FAO) has attemped to standardize the names of all the commercial shrimp in the world in English, French, and Spanish. Following the FAO lead, this book will stick to the name *shrimp*, with two exceptions. One is for the cultured freshwater prawn (see page 7), which is given as an alternative in some recipes (and is known as a prawn in the FAO lists). The other exception is more personal and less rational: a few Asian dishes such as Salt and Pepper Prawns (see page 82) are so commonly found on restaurant menus that the names just don't sound right any other way.

Shrimp Species

Although shrimp classification can be complicated, for most purposes we can refer to two main categories: warm-water (*penaeid*) species and cold-water (*caridean*) shrimp.

Any shrimp in the shell can be readily identified as one or the other by looking at the first and second shell segments covering the abdomen (see Anatomy of a Shrimp, page 11). In warm-water shrimp, the first segment overlaps the second, the second the third, and so on to the tail. In cold-water species, the second segment overlaps both the first and third. Why bother with such a minute point of anatomy? Because the two types are not always interchangeable in use.

WARM-WATER SPECIES Warm-water shrimp, found all around the tropics and in most subtropical waters, make up approximately 80 percent of world shrimp consumption. Virtually all of the frozen raw shrimp in the market are of this type. There are dozens of commercial species of warm-water shrimp, but for our purposes I group

*Warm-water shrimp.
Clockwise from top: royal
red shrimp* (Pleoticus
robustus), *Alabama; white
shrimp* (Penaeus setiferus),
Mexico; white shrimp
(Penaeus setiferus), *Florida;
cultured white shrimp*
(Penaeus chinensis), *China;
pink "hopper" shrimp*
(Penaeus duorarum),
*Florida; cultured black
tiger shrimp* (Penaeus
monodon), *Thailand.*

them into four main types: white, brown, pink, and tiger.

Despite these names, color is not a very useful way of distinguishing one variety from another. Shrimp vary in appearance even within a single species, and "white" shrimp come in a range of colors including pink, green, purplish, and blue-gray, some of them darker than other species classified as "brown" shrimp. (All species turn pink when cooked.) Rather than specifying color, shrimp processors group the various species according to other traits, including subtle anatomical differences, preferred habitat, and feeding habits. The last trait is probably the most important to the cook, because it has the greatest effect on the flavor of the shrimp.

White shrimp generally command the highest prices in the United States. They make up about one-third of the domestic warm-water shrimp catch along the south Atlantic and Gulf coasts and constitute a major part of the Mexican Gulf fishery. The peak season for fresh white Gulf shrimp is August to December. Related white shrimp species are found along the Pacific coast from Mexico to Peru, where they are both caught in the wild and cultured (see Shrimp Farming, page 8). Chinese white shrimp are relative newcomers to our shores, but they are now being farmed on a large scale on China's northeastern coast and will be increasingly important in the world market.

All the white shrimp have certain traits in common. You can distinguish them from browns and pinks by the smooth, rather than ridged, final tail segment. More importantly, they are mainly herbivorous, which gives them a milder flavor than other varieties.

Brown shrimp are more common than whites; one Gulf species constitutes more than half of all domestic warm-water shrimp landings. Another species of brown shrimp from the west coast of Mexico sometimes makes up as much as half of the annual Mexican shrimp landings. Although Americans prefer whites overall, brown shrimp are more popular in certain areas, notably Texas. As in the case of white shrimp, the color varies by species and by habitat, but all brown shrimp have a distinctive ridge on the tail, with a groove on either side. Brown shrimp are omnivorous, feeding on microscopic animals (zooplankton) as well as algae, which gives them a slightly stronger flavor than whites. They occasionally have a noticeable iodine flavor and aroma. The peak season for fresh Gulf browns is from June to October.

Pink shrimp are the least common of the three major species of domestic shrimp, making up less than 15 percent of the catch. The pink, or "hopper," shrimp caught off western and southern Florida are among my favorites; they live in deeper waters than the others and feed almost entirely on zooplankton, giving them an especially sweet flavor. They are mostly caught from October to May, a time when browns and whites are less common.

Tiger shrimp (or tiger prawns, as they are often called) are native to the western Pacific and Indian oceans. There are several species of tiger-striped shrimp in that part of the world, but the giant tiger prawn is the most common commercial species and the one most widely cultured. Tigers are especially attractive, both raw and cooked; when cooked, the shells turn bright orange, keeping their characteristic stripes. The meat also has an especially strong orange color when cooked. However, flavor and texture vary from one source to another; some of the less expensive tigers have a somewhat gummy texture, especially when cooked by moist-heat methods.

Other warm-water shrimp species notable for their flavor include the royal red shrimp of the Gulf of Mexico, a deepwater species with a sweet-salty flavor, sold mainly individually quick frozen, and the Pacific blue shrimp, which in its Hawaiian cultured version is hands down the sweetest shrimp I have ever tasted.

Two other warm-water varieties, the rock shrimp of Florida and the West Coast ridgeback shrimp, are dealt with under Miscellaneous Species (page 7).

COLD-WATER SPECIES The northern oceans of the world produce several species of generally small shrimp, collectively known as cold-water shrimp or carids. By far the majority of the commercial carid catch is sold in cooked and peeled form, but a few species show up fresh from time to time in local markets.

Freezer boats—which are often giant floating factories equipped to catch, cook, peel, devein, and package shrimp at sea—work the northern Atlantic, Pacific, and Arctic oceans for small cold-water shrimp to be sold as cooked and peeled "salad" or "bay" shrimp. The latter term is especially popular on the West Coast, and many a diner at San Francisco's Fisherman's Wharf may be under the illusion that the shellfish in his Shrimp Louis came out of the nearby bay. Alas, it didn't, and hasn't for at least the past forty years. San Francisco Bay used to support a commercial fishery for a small cold-water species, *Crangon franciscorum*, but it was fished out by the 1950s. Although the name "bay shrimp" persists, it generally applies to one species or another of *Pandalus* caught in the deeper waters of the north Pacific.

As is true of raw warm-water shrimp, cooked cold-water shrimp vary in quality. With both, your best bet is to find a dealer who has a good product and stick with it.

A few larger carid species from the Pacific are sold fresh in major West Coast urban markets. One is spot shrimp, found from central California to Alaska. In California, they are generally sold as "Monterey prawns," and most of the limited catch goes to restaurants. Females are often caught with a cluster of eggs on the underside of the tail; while the roe does not contribute much flavor, it turns bright red in cooking and makes an attractive garnish for sauces. Other cold-water varieties sold fresh include sidestripe and coonstripe shrimp, both found from Washington to Alaska.

Because these large cold-water varieties tend to inhabit rocky reefs rather than open seafloor, they are caught in traps rather than the trawl nets used for other species. The supply will always be limited, but they are delicious and definitely worth trying if you find some in the market. In my experience, they are best when cooked by dry heat (grilled in the shell, broiled, or sautéed); steamed or poached, they can come out mushy.

*An assortment of shrimp species and forms. Center: freshwater prawn (*Macro- brachium rosenbergii*), Thailand. Upper right: two thick-shelled varieties, peeled raw Florida rock shrimp (*Sicyonia brevirostris*) and whole California ridgeback shrimp (*Sicyonia ingentis*). Lower left: spot shrimp (*Pandalus platyceros*), a typical large Pacific cold-water species. Two types of cooked and peeled shrimp: lower right, small northern shrimp (*Pandalus borealis*); left, cultured Thai tiger shrimp (*Penaeus monodon*).*

MISCELLANEOUS SPECIES Although a number of species of shrimplike creatures are found in fresh water around the world, only one is of commercial importance. The giant river prawn, *Macrobrachium rosenbergii*, is native to the rivers and estuaries of Southeast Asia, where it is the predominant shellfish in inland areas. It is cultured all over the region and in Hawaii and is being raised experimentally in other countries. In addition to the tail meat, there is a tasty morsel of meat inside each large claw. Dry-heat cooking methods are preferable to moist heat for this species.

There is no reason to buy freshwater prawns if all you will use is the tail; save them for occasions when you can take advantage of their striking appearance, as in the variation on Dancing Prawns (see page 34).

Although technically warm-water shrimp, two commercial species are sufficiently different from the penaeids to be placed in a separate family. More important to the cook, they have especially heavy shells that make peeling difficult, so they have developed special market niches. One is the rock shrimp of the southern Atlantic and Gulf coasts, *Sicyonia brevirostris*. Until a special peeling machine was developed to remove its tough, thick shell, this species was routinely discarded. Now it is an important commercial species, mainly from Florida.

The peeled raw tail meat is available both fresh and frozen. (In California I have seen it sold as "stir-fry shrimp," and it is excellent for that purpose.) The rather stubby peeled tails are round rather than oval in cross-section, with red and white markings on the surface. The flavor is almost lobsterlike and noticeably salty. When using rock shrimp in place of other raw shrimp, reduce the salt in the recipe.

The West Coast counterpart of rock shrimp is the small ridgeback shrimp or ridgeback prawn, *Sicyonia ingentis*. Caught mainly off the Channel Islands of southern California, it has developed a strong local following. You can use the peeled tail meat in place of other peeled shrimp, but most often the species is steamed as a "peel and eat" appetizer.

Shrimp Farming

With most wild shrimp stocks currently being fished to their capacity, the only way to satisfy the growing world demand for shrimp is to raise them. In the last decade, shrimp aquaculture, or farming, has gone from an experimental process for raising warm-water shrimp to a major component of the shrimp industry. By 1990, farms are expected to supply one-third of all warm-water shrimp sold worldwide and one-quarter of the total shrimp market.

Farmed shrimp are comparable in both quality and price to frozen "wild" shrimp of the same varieties. I know of no way to tell by looking at a pile of thawed shrimp if they are wild or farmed, unless the species makes it obvious. (Some types, such as black tiger shrimp from Asia and freshwater *Macrobrachium* prawns, are only available farmed.)

Shrimp reproduce by means of eggs, which warm-water shrimp release into the ocean to hatch. After the eggs hatch, the larvae drift toward shore and into estuaries, natural "nurseries" where they grow into the postlarval juvenile stage. In nature, the juveniles migrate to open salt water to mature into adults.

The simplest method of shrimp culture, known as extensive aquaculture, requires only a way of controlling the water flow in and out of shallow coastal ponds. When juvenile shrimp are abundant in inshore waters, shrimp farmers simply open a gate and allow the sea to flow into the enclosure, bringing in millions of the tiny creatures. The gates are then closed, trapping the shrimp inside. The tide brings nutrients and flushes away wastes (screens in the outlets prevent the shrimp from being washed out with the out-going tide), and those shrimp that survive to maturity are easily harvested with nets. Survival rates are not as high as with other methods of shrimp farming, but capitalization and energy costs are kept to a minimum, making this the type of shrimp aquaculture most common in developing countries.

Extensive aquaculture has been practiced in some areas for centuries. The Inca of South America were harvesting shrimp by this method 400 years ago. Ecuador's modern shrimp farmers rediscovered the technique by accident in 1962 when unusually high tides broke through a levee, flooding a coastal coconut plantation. By the time the farmer was able to repair the levee and drain the field, he had a substantial crop of shrimp.

By adding more equipment and energy to the system, farmers can construct artificial ponds on nearby dry land, pumping fresh seawater in and out as needed. This semi-intensive form of aquaculture may use wild, tide-borne larvae or hatchery-bred stock (either produced on-site or purchased from separate hatcheries); typically, there are separate nursery and growout ponds and a supplemental food supply. A semi-intensive farm can produce two to ten times as much shrimp per acre as a simple coastal impoundment. Most of the dramatic increase in shrimp exports from Latin America (especially Ecuador) in the 1980s has come from new semi-intensive farms.

Intensive aquaculture requires the greatest investment of capital and energy, but produces still higher yields. The growing environment is much more controlled, with water filtration and aeration allowing much higher densities of shrimp than could survive in extensive or semi-intensive ponds. Japan and Taiwan, where land is especially scarce, lead the world in intensive shrimp aquaculture. One intensive farm in Hawaii uses greenhouse-like covered concrete raceways, producing more than a thousand times as much shrimp per acre of water as typical extensive ponds.

Nutritional Profile

Shrimp meat is approximately 18 percent protein and less than 1 percent fat. A 100-gram serving (about 3½ ounces) of raw shrimp delivers 91 calories, most of it from protein. (In calculating nutritional values of foods, 100 grams is the standard serving.) Shrimp is a good source of phosphorus (166 milligrams per serving), potassium (220 mg), and niacin (3.2 mg) and a modest source of calcium (63 mg). Of the small amount of fat in shrimp, up to one-third is of the beneficial omega-3 polyunsaturated variety, which has been shown to reduce the risk of heart disease.

The one nutritional drawback of shrimp is that it is relatively high in cholesterol. A 100-gram serving of warm-water shrimp contains between 125 and 150 milligrams of cholesterol, depending on the species; cold-water shrimp run around 125 mg in a 100-gram serving. By comparison, lean beef, pork, veal, lamb, and chicken are all in the range of 65 to 80 mg per serving. A single egg yolk contains 213 mg. Nutritionists recommend that healthy adults consume no more than 300 mg of dietary cholesterol per day; a single serving of shrimp can provide half that amount. Clearly, filling up on shrimp day after day is not a good idea.

However, your body's absorption of dietary cholesterol is affected by the amount and type of fats you eat. Saturated fats, including butterfat and other animal fats plus certain tropical oils, tend to increase the dangers of cholesterol, while omega-3 fats (found chiefly in seafood) and monounsaturated fats (found in olive oil and certain other vegetable oils) decrease its harmful effects.

Some, but by no means all, of the recipes in this book have been designed to minimize cholesterol and saturated fat. Sometimes nothing can match the flavor and texture that butter, cream, or eggs bring to a dish. Just remember that daily fluctuations are not as important as overall patterns, and a day of indulgence is best followed by a day of leaner meals. In short, unless you are on a severely cholesterol-restricted diet for medical reasons, shrimp is an ideal part of a balanced and varied diet.

Shopping for Shrimp

Frozen shrimp are available both raw and cooked in supermarkets and fish markets all across the country. Unlike fresh shrimp, which are seasonal, frozen shrimp are available throughout the year at consistent prices. With all the diversity of sources, species, and sizes, prices vary considerably, so shop around. If you want to buy in quantity, check with seafood wholesalers in your area to see if they will sell to individuals on a "cash and carry" basis.

Because shrimp are used so often in Asian cuisines, chances are you will find the greatest variety and the best retail prices in Asian markets. In my experience, Chinatown retail prices are often comparable to wholesale prices, and the hours are more convenient. (Wholesalers open very early and usually close by midafternoon.)

Product Forms

FRESH It would be easy to state, as many books do, that virtually all the shrimp sold in North America is frozen. But it would neither be true nor do justice to those seafood purveyors all over the country who make special efforts to obtain the best possible fresh products for their customers.

Until recently, fresh shrimp has been a local phenomenon limited to port cities. With so much of the industry, from the boats to the retail counters and restaurant kitchens, geared to a frozen product, little attention has been given to providing never-frozen shrimp beyond the local area.

But the situation is changing. In a number of American cities, alliances of (mostly) young restaurant chefs and the quality-obsessed wholesalers who supply them have gone to great lengths to supply a demanding clientele with fresh shrimp. In Berkeley, California, where I live, there is a retail fish market that sometimes has three types of fresh shrimp at a time. There are not only fresh West Coast varieties such as spot shrimp or sidestripes from Alaska and ridgebacks from Santa Barbara, but once or twice a week in season there are magnificently fresh pink hopper shrimp flown in from Apalachicola, Florida.

If you really like shrimp, you owe it to yourself to seek out those restaurants and shops that sell it fresh. This is especially true if you live near or travel to shrimp fishing areas along the Atlantic, Gulf, and Pacific coasts. In other areas, thanks to a growing air-freight seafood distribution network, fish dealers in most major cities have access to fresh shrimp within hours after they are landed.

Those dealers who do go to the trouble to get fresh shrimp will undoubtedly feature the word *fresh* on the label. Labeling laws vary by state and locality, but in most areas seafood cannot be labeled fresh if it has been frozen at any time. If it has been frozen, the label usually says something like "previously frozen," "thawed," or my favorite concoction, "frozen fresh thawed." (I never understood the term *fresh frozen*, which fortunately is becoming less common; it should go without saying that seafood is frozen while still fresh, not just before it spoils.)

Of course, "fresh" in the sense of "never frozen" does not automatically guarantee better quality (although it does practically guarantee a higher price). Fresh shrimp that have sat for days in a refrigerator are no longer fresh. Learn to judge for yourself the quality of any shrimp, whether fresh, frozen, or thawed (see page 12).

FROZEN Most of the shrimp most of us eat has been frozen, and frozen shrimp is, by and large, an excellent product. Still, quality varies from one species, source, or season to the next.

Block freezing is far and away the most common form of preserving raw shrimp. A measured weight of shrimp in the shell, either with heads or headless, is packed into a clear plastic bag inside a carton. Water is added to the bag to completely surround the shrimp; when frozen, the water forms a glaze which protects the shrimp from changes in temperature and dehydration. Block-frozen shrimp are good for several years if properly stored, and the solid, compact shape of the packages is easy to handle. However, the entire package (typically two to five pounds) must be thawed before any of the shrimp can be used, and the remainder cannot be refrozen for long.

The other method of freezing shrimp is individually quick frozen (IQF). In this technique, individual shrimp are frozen and then glazed by dipping in or spraying with water and refreezing, sometimes several times. They are then packed rather loosely into bags that fit into cartons. The advantage of IQF shrimp is that you can thaw as many shrimp as you need and keep the rest frozen for future use. However, because of their thinner glaze, IQF shrimp are more susceptible to freezer burn than block-frozen shrimp, making their freezer shelf life shorter.

IQF shrimp with shells on would seem to be an ideal product from the consumer's standpoint, but so far the supply has been limited. The limiting factor may be a distribution system geared to long freezer storage. (IQF shrimp have a maximum shelf life of about 6 months, versus years for block-frozen.) But a huge IQF facility is now under construction near the principal shrimp farming area in mainland China, so we may see an increasing amount of IQF shell-on shrimp from China in the years to come.

For now, peeled and deveined IQF raw shrimp is more common. Although this seems like the most convenient form of all — no shells, no veins, no waste — I have not been impressed with the quality of frozen peeled shrimp and I rarely use it.

COOKED The small to tiny *Pandalus* and *Crangon* shrimp from the colder northern oceans of the world are almost always sold cooked. The most common form is peeled and deveined tails, variously known as "bay shrimp," "shrimp meat," or just plain "shrimp" (to distinguish them from "prawns"). Some come in IQF form, some packed into cans and frozen, but they are almost always sold in thawed form. Like other shrimp, they vary according to source and species; some are quite flavorful and relatively firm, while others are soft to the point of mushiness and blandly sweet. There is no way to tell without tasting them, so buy from a supplier you trust. If there is a person behind the fish counter, it can't hurt to ask for a taste.

To confuse matters further, the same species are sometimes sold in unpeeled form as cold-water prawns. While they are attractive — about the size of a half dollar with tightly curled tails, smooth pink shells, and black eyes — the meat tends to be soft. I have never found a use for them where freshly cooked warm-water shrimp or tiny cooked and peeled shrimp did not work better. They are, however, quite inexpensive.

Cooked warm-water shrimp are becoming increasingly common, mainly in IQF peeled and deveined form. These can run to rather large sizes, and if you just have to have a shrimp cocktail but don't want to cook, they are convenient.

DRIED Salting and drying in the sun is a traditional method of preserving shrimp. Dried shrimp are especially popular as a seasoning in Asia and Latin America. Only one recipe in this book calls for them (see Shrimp Cakes, page 66).

Anatomy of a Shrimp

Shrimp are invertebrates, meaning they lack a backbone and internal skeleton. Instead, like other crustaceans, they maintain their shape by means of an exoskeleton (shell) made up of many segments.

The two major sections of a shrimp's body, what we commonly call the "head" and "tail," are more properly known as the cephalothorax and the abdomen. The former is covered by a large single piece of shell known as the carapace and contains the eyes, mouth, and other headlike parts, as well as the gills, most of the digestive system, and virtually all of the fat in the animal. The carapace typically has a long, pointed extension above the mouth known as the rostrum, which varies in length by species. The only reason cooks need to know about the rostrum is that it is sharp. All this is routinely removed from most shrimp by simply breaking the shrimp in half where the head joins the tail.

Virtually all of the edible meat in a shrimp is in the curved abdomen, or "tail." Shrimp have multiple pairs of small legs, which they use to swim or move about on the bottom of the sea. But when they need to move quickly, say to escape from a predator, they flex their relatively large abdominal muscles, and scoot backward with quick pulses. This abdominal muscle tissue is the "meat" of the shrimp.

Running down the center of the abdomen on the dorsal (upper or outer) side is the intestinal tube, euphemistically called the "sand vein" or just plain "vein." This tube carries waste products from the shrimp's digestive system out through an opening at the tail end. While the vein and its contents are harmless, many cooks prefer to "devein" shrimp for aesthetic reasons (see Deveining, page 14). The real vein, which is part of the circulatory system, is a much thinner tube running along the ventral (inner or under) side of the tail, and it does not have to be removed.

Sizes

Adjectives such as small, medium, large, and jumbo do not convey the same meaning to everyone, so the shrimp industry classifies shrimp by the number of pieces per pound. The various families of shrimp range from enormous freshwater prawns, which can approach a pound apiece, to tiny oceanic krill, which run into the hundreds per pound. Most commercial shell-on shrimp fall into the range of 10 to 70 per pound; smaller shrimp are typically sold cooked and peeled.

To ensure uniformity in sizes, virtually all the frozen shrimp in the U.S. market are sold in size-sorted form, expressed as a count per pound. Some years ago, the U.S. government came up with a system of descriptive names for each of the commercial size categories (see table). Bigger being better in the American mind, the scale is weighted heavily toward the larger sizes, resulting in such comical names as Extra Jumbo shrimp.

SIZE NAME	COUNT per lb.
Extra Colossal	Under 10
Colossal	10–15
Extra Jumbo	16–20
Jumbo	21–25
Extra Large	26–30
Large	31–35
Medium Large	36–40
Medium	41–50
Small	51–60
Extra small	61–70
Tiny	Over 70

No market is likely to carry shrimp in all the sizes listed in the table. In fact, I have never seen the labels Colossal or Extra Colossal in use, even in markets that sell those sizes. The names in general use are Jumbo, Large (occasionally Extra Large), and Medium. (Nobody wants to admit that he is selling small shrimp.) Some markets have begun to add the count per pound to their labels, making it clear exactly what size they are offering.

For the purpose of the recipes in this book, I have used four size categories:

Small means 41–50 or 51–60 count (shrimp per pound); these are ideal for soups, gumbos, pasta sauces, and other dishes in which you want a piece of shrimp in nearly every bite. They are typically the least expensive, but are often available only in Asian or other ethnic markets. The savings are at a slight cost in texture; smaller shrimp will never be as firm and meaty as the largest sizes, although the flavor is still excellent.

Medium (31–35 or 36–40 count) is the most versatile size and the next-best bargain. These are generally the smallest shrimp sold in mainstream supermarkets and fish markets, and they are suitable for stir-fried and sautéed dishes, shrimp cocktails and other cold preparations, and even grilling in the shell.

Large refers to the 21–25 or 26–30 sizes. These are the larger of the two sizes of "prawns" found in most West Coast markets. Choose them when you want a more impressive effect, as in showy cocktails or certain sautéed dishes, or when you want a larger platform for stuffings.

Jumbos (16–20 and larger) are, quite frankly, overpriced. True, they produce the firmest, sweetest meat, but they are in such demand by the restaurant trade that under-10 shrimp may be up to three times the price per pound of 41–50s from the same source. The reason has to do with both perceived quality and labor costs; it takes as much time to peel and devein a small shrimp as a large one, so restaurants would rather serve 4 or 5 shrimp than a dozen or more. The same principle applies to home cooks; choose larger shrimp to save time, smaller sizes to save money.

If buying whole shrimp (those with their heads on), bear in mind that the count per pound includes the weight of the head, which is about 30 percent of the total weight. Thus the size of the tails is smaller than the count would suggest. A pound of 16–20 head-on tiger prawns, for example, contains approximately 18 pieces. When the heads

are removed, the yield is about 11 ounces of tails. Thus the tails themselves run about 26 to the pound.

Judging Quality

Whether shrimp are sold fresh or thawed, learn to judge their quality for yourself. You can make some of the following checks at the market. If you don't feel comfortable asking to take a close look or to sniff a batch of shrimp in the store, then check the shrimp when you get home. If they are not up to standard, return them immediately for a refund.

APPEARANCE The shrimp should be uniform in color, with no physical damage to the shells or meat. (Shrimp with a noticeable amount of broken pieces should sell at a discount price.) Raw shell-on shrimp sometimes show irregular black spots on the shells; this condition, known as melanosis, occurs because of a natural enzyme reaction to sunlight. It is not in itself a problem, but it may indicate a delay in icing the shrimp after they were caught. Sulfites are sometimes added to shrimp to prevent melanosis; under federal law, packages so treated must be labeled "sulfites added as a preservative."

In head-on shrimp, blackening around the gill area (under the carapace just in front of the abdomen) is often the first sign of spoilage. If the heads are removed at or before this point, the tails may have another day of shelf life; if the heads are left on, the spoilage will spread quickly.

Block-frozen shrimp should be solid, with every piece covered by at least a thin layer of ice. Exposed shrimp indicate that the block has thawed at least partially. Avoid packages with opaque white patches in the meat or whitened, partially detached shells; these too are signs that the glaze has failed, producing a dessicated condition known as "freezer burn." IQF packages should not have a lot of ice crystals in the bag, a sign of thawing and refreezing.

AROMA Shrimp should have a pleasant "sea breeze" or seaweed-like aroma. Any detectable fishy or ammonia odor (a sign of bacterial decomposition) means the shrimp are too old and should be discarded. Another bad odor that

I have heard of but never experienced is a petroleum smell from leakage of oil or fuel from the boat's bilge into the hold where shrimp are stored. A slight iodine odor is characteristic of certain species. Unless it is overpowering it is not a flaw.

TEXTURE Raw or cooked, shrimp should be firm and moist (although they will of course be firmer after cooking). Most textural problems do not show up until after the shrimp are cooked, which in a sense is too late. However, even if you cannot return the shrimp to the store, let the retailer know about the flaw.

If not caused by overcooking, a tough, dry, or fibrous texture in frozen shrimp can come from storing the shrimp too long or at fluctuating temperatures. Mushy meat is a sign of some spoilage prior to freezing, probably due to delays in chilling the catch. A chalky texture comes from delay in removing the heads, which gives the digestive juices of the shrimp a chance to begin breaking down the meat. An extremely chewy, rubbery texture can come from overuse of sodium tripolyphosphate, an additive used by some processors to control moisture loss during freezing and thawing.

How Much To Buy?

Most of the recipes in this book get three to four main-course servings out of a pound of raw shell-on shrimp. A pound of shell-on tails will yield about 14 ounces (400 grams) of raw shrimp meat, or 3½ ounces (100 grams) per serving. According to most nutrition authorities, 100 grams of boneless meat or seafood supplies all the protein the average adult needs per day, although many of us regularly eat more. Because cooked and peeled shrimp have shrunk somewhat in the cooking process, about 3 ounces supply the nutritional equivalent of 3½ ounces of raw peeled shrimp.

If you are buying shrimp with the heads on, you will need an extra 40 to 50 percent to get the equivalent weight in tails. The heads cost just as much to process and ship as the tails, so unless the price per pound is less than two-thirds that of the equivalent size of tails, you are not saving money by buying the heads. In general, buy head-on shrimp only when you have a use for the heads (as in a bisque), when you want them for the sake of presentation, or when the shrimp are sold only that way, as is the case with some fresh local shrimp.

If you can use them in sufficient quantity, a whole box of block-frozen shrimp can be a good buy. Asian markets may be your best bet for finding a selection of frozen shrimp. One warning, however: some imported shrimp are packaged in 2-kilogram (4.4-pound) boxes, which look very similar to 5-pound boxes. If you are not careful, you may end up paying more per pound for the frozen shrimp by the box than for the same shrimp thawed at the fish counter!

Be especially wary if the weight marked on the box appears to have been modified. In one instance, 2-kilo boxes erroneously labeled "net weight 5 pounds" were corrected with a price sticker reading "net weight 4.4 pounds." I saw some "5-pound" boxes for sale which looked suspiciously as if a stick-on label had been removed. Sure enough, just down the street another store was selling identical boxes labeled with the corrected weight over the incorrect figure.

Preparation

Unless you buy them already peeled and deveined, shrimp require some simple preparation before cooking.

THAWING Most shrimp are sold already thawed, but if you buy a whole box you will need to thaw it yourself. Block-frozen shrimp are best thawed overnight in the refrigerator. Discard the box and inside plastic wrapper and place the block of frozen shrimp in a colander set inside a large bowl or on a cooling rack set inside a roasting pan. The shrimp should not sit in their own juices as they thaw.

If you are in a hurry, a block will thaw in an hour or so when submerged in cold or just barely lukewarm water. There is no need to run water over them constantly; just change the water every 15 minutes or so. By that time the shrimp will have cooled the water so much that it won't be thawing them very quickly. Remove shrimp from the block as they float free, and drain them in a colander. (Do not pull them loose too soon or you may damage the shells.)

Avoid letting thawed shrimp soak in water for a long time; they may become waterlogged. In theory, you can thaw just as many shrimp as you need from a block this way and return the rest to the freezer. However, the temperature of the block will have risen to the point that you should plan on cooking the shrimp within a week.

IQF shrimp (see page 10) should be thawed without water, in the refrigerator. Just give them a quick rinse after thawing, drain, and they are ready to cook (if raw) or serve (if cooked).

STORING For the best possible flavor, keep shrimp cold and don't keep them long. If possible, buy shrimp on the day you will cook them. However, freshly thawed shrimp will keep for a day or longer in the refrigerator. Rinse them and drain well after arriving home and place them in a covered container, with a paper towel on the bottom to absorb any drippings.

Fresh head-on shrimp are more perishable than tails; by the second day they may show some blackening around the gills, the first sign of spoilage. If you can't use them the day you buy them, remove the heads and freeze them for a Shrimp Bisque (see page 54), Quick Shrimp Stock (page 113), or Shrimp Butter (page 112). The tails can keep until a second or even third day.

Once thawed, shrimp should not be refrozen because the texture will suffer badly. If bought frozen and not allowed to thaw on the way home, frozen shrimp may be kept for weeks or even months in a good-sized freezer capable of holding a temperature near 0° F. However, the smaller your freezer and the more often you open it, the shorter the life of frozen foods will be.

PEELING Although it is possible to eat shrimp shell and all (especially the smaller sizes), most of the time peeling is in order. The following instructions are illustrated with raw shrimp, but the procedure is the same for cooked shrimp.

Holding the shrimp by the tail end, pull off the legs and shell segments on the ventral side (fig. 1).

The upper shell segments now lift away easily (fig. 2). If you want to leave the last section of the shell (sometimes called the "tail feathers") attached, perhaps as a handle for battering and frying, carefully crack and peel the last seg-

fig. 1

fig. 2

ment so only the branched part of the tail is still encased in its shell. Unless this method is specified, peeled shrimp in the recipes should be completely peeled.

DEVEINING Before I discuss how to devein shrimp, there is the question of whether or not to do so. Sometimes

14

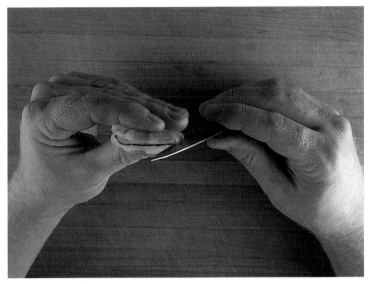

fig. 3

fig. 4

and eat" boiled or steamed shrimp are popular, most people don't bother with deveining. Still, if the thought of eating the last stage of the shrimp's digestive system offends you, by all means devein.

Personally, I decide on each batch of shrimp by cutting open and inspecting a few of them. If the veins seem especially dirty, I devein them, but if the first few have next to nothing in their veins, I assume the rest are equally clean and cook them as is.

To devein a peeled shrimp, hold it by the sides and make a narrow cut along the length of the dorsal side to expose the vein (fig. 3). Lift or scrape out the vein (fig. 4) and rinse the shrimp.

There is a special tool that peels and deveins shrimp with one stroke. You insert it at the head end and push it toward the tail end, and it cuts a groove to expose the vein as it forces the shell off (fig. 5). These tools come in several designs; two are shown here. The yellow one is sold by seafood distributor Slade Gorton Co. of Boston, the stainless steel version through the Williams-Sonoma mail-order catalog. Follow the manufacturer's directions carefully, especially regarding the position of the shrimp (straight or curved). Neither tool does the job as neatly as a knife. If perfectly uniform appearance is important, as in a shrimp cocktail, use the knife method.

fig. 5

the contents of the vein can be gritty, which makes for an unpleasant texture if eaten. More often, it is just a matter of perceived cleanliness. People who gleefully eat the entire contents of a clam or oyster shell get inexplicably squeamish about eating shrimp that have not been deveined. In many parts of the South, especially where "peel

fig. 6

Several recipes in this book call for deveining shrimp to be cooked in their shells. To devein through the shell, cut open the shell along the dorsal curve with small scissors (fig. 6), or cut *outward* with a small knife (holding the shrimp down against the cutting board is the easiest and safest way to do this). I have seen recipes instructing cooks to cut through shrimp shells from the outside with a knife, which is as sure a way of cutting your fingers as I can imagine. Remove the vein and rinse as for peeled shrimp.

CUTTING This book calls for a few special cuts: butterflying, splitting, and dicing. To butterfly shrimp, peel as directed above, leaving the tail shells on. Make the deveining cut deeper, almost all the way through to the ventral side; devein and fold the sides out flat (fig. 7).

Splitting a peeled shrimp entirely in half lengthwise (fig. 8) yields two pieces. This gives you twice as many pieces of shrimp in the finished dish, and the halves curl into attractive spirals as they cook.

A few recipes call for diced shrimp. Simply cut the peeled and deveined shrimp crosswise into pieces roughly as long as they are thick.

SALT-LEACHING Several years ago, when I was buying shrimp in a Chinatown market which had half a

dozen varieties and sizes on display, the fishmonger told me that the shrimp I had chosen needed to be soaked in salted water before cooking. I was in a hurry and didn't have time to ask why, but tucked his advice back in a deep corner of my memory.

Recently, I came across instructions for salt-leaching in the book *Chinese Technique* by Ken Hom and Harvey

fig. 7

fig. 8

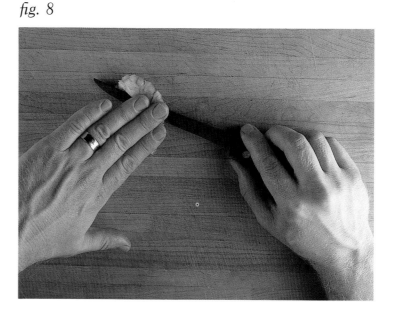

16

Steiman (Simon and Schuster). Hom explains that salting peeled shrimp prior to cooking "cuts through the sticky film, makes the shrimp crunchy, and gives them a glossy cast . . . and a cleaner taste." I tried it, and now I use his salt-leaching method for any shrimp to be sautéed or stir-fried. (It seems to have little effect on shrimp cooked by other methods.) The salt draws out excess moisture. As long as you don't leave the salt on too long, there is no time for it to soak into the shrimp. Smaller frozen shrimp especially benefit from this technique, becoming noticeably firmer without being tough.

To salt-leach shrimp, sprinkle them with 2 teaspoons kosher salt per pound, toss to distribute the salt evenly, and let stand 1 minute. Rinse and drain. Repeat. Drain well and transfer to a small bowl. The shrimp are now ready for cooking or for additional marinades.

Notes to the Cook

SHRIMP Unless specified otherwise in the recipes, *shrimp* means raw, headless tails, in the shell. Sizes follow the general ranges listed on page 12 unless a more specific size is indicated. In some recipes where the amount of shrimp is not crucial to the texture or flavor of the dish, the ingredients list may give a quantity such as "1 to 1½ pounds"; let your appetite be your guide.

SERVING SIZES are for average appetites, with appetizers and first courses meant to precede another course. However, many of the dishes in the First Courses chapter are also suitable for fewer servings as a main dish, and half portions of some of the recipes in the Entrées chapter could precede another main course of meat, poultry, or seafood.

BUTTER in this book means unsalted butter. If using salted butter or margarine, remember to decrease the salt elsewhere in the recipe.

CHILES Several of the recipes call for small fresh chiles. I use mostly the Mexican *chile serrano*, 2 to 3 inches long and about ⅜ inch thick. The somewhat larger jalapeño and Fresno chiles are less hot, so they can be substi-

tuted piece for piece. All three are sometimes available as red (fully ripe) chiles; the ripeness does not affect their heat but adds a bit of sweetness in addition to color. The tiny Asian "bird" or "bird's eye" chiles are just too hot for my taste to be very useful. With any chiles, removing the seeds and ribs makes them much less hot. Remember to wash your hands promptly after handling chiles, and don't touch your eyes or other sensitive areas.

OIL When no other oil (such as olive or sesame) is specified, use a neutral-tasting vegetable oil with a high smoking point. Peanut oil is ideal; corn, safflower, and cottonseed oils are also acceptable.

SALT Many recipes call for "salt to taste," even at points in the recipe when it is clearly not appropriate to taste the dish. What is meant is to add salt according to your own experience and taste. Most of us have a sense of how much salt is enough for a given number of servings. Learn to season as professional cooks do, by feel and by eye—whether in pinches between the fingertips or shakes from a shaker. If in doubt, use less salt and add more later if needed.

The recipes in this book were developed with kosher salt, which is coarser and less salty per teaspoon than table salt. If using table salt, start with half as much as called for (when measured amounts of salt are indicated), then adjust to taste.

Appetizers

Shrimp and Fresh Corn Tamales

Basic Steamed Shrimp

This is my favorite method of cooking shrimp for salads and other cold dishes or when they will be flavored further as in Shrimp in Beer (see page 36). Cooking the shrimp in the shell preserves flavors that would otherwise be lost, and keeps the shrimp firm. The ginger and rice wine do not really linger in the shrimp; instead, they preserve and support its natural flavor. The result is compatible with Asian and Western seasonings.

1 pound shrimp, deveined in the shell (see page 16)
Kosher salt
5 or 6 slices fresh ginger
3 tablespoons dry sherry or Chinese rice wine

1. For steaming, you will need some way of supporting a shallow bowl over boiling water under a cover. One solution is a deep, wide kettle or wok with a flat steaming rack. Another is a special Chinese-style steamer, either the all-metal type with its own pot underneath or the bamboo steaming baskets that sit on top of a wok. Whichever you use, the diameter of the pot or steamer tray must be large enough that you can retrieve the bowl while wearing oven mitts (to protect your hands from the steam).

2. Rinse and drain the shrimp and place them in a shallow bowl that will fit inside your steamer. Sprinkle with a little salt, then add the ginger and wine. Fill the steaming pot with water to a depth of at least 1 inch, but below the level of the steaming rack. Bring to a rolling boil, add the shrimp in its bowl, cover, and steam until the shells turn pink and the meat is opaque white, 5 to 8 minutes depending on size. Drain the shrimp well, but do not rinse. Allow them to cool before peeling if peeled shrimp are called for in the recipe you're making. Steamed shrimp will keep up to a day in the refrigerator, tightly covered.

Variation The one disadvantage of the previous method is that shrimp cooked in the shell do not curl as tightly as they do when peeled first. When shape is important, as for Shrimp Cocktail (see page 45), I use a different method. Omit the seasonings and peel and devein the shrimp, leaving the tail shells on if desired. Fit a covered saucepan with a steaming rack that will hold the shrimp above boiling water. Bring at least 1 inch of water to a rolling boil, place the shrimp on the rack, cover, and steam until the meat is fully opaque, 4 to 7 minutes depending on size. Remove the shrimp immediately and spread them out on a plate or tray to cool. Chill until ready to serve.

Shrimp Rémoulade

In classic French cooking, *sauce rémoulade* is a mayonnaise flavored with mustard, anchovy, pickles, capers, and herbs (see Rémoulade Sauce I, page 110). But Shrimp Rémoulade is a Louisiana Creole dish and, as they so often do, Creole cooks have developed their own piquant variation on the French original (see Rémoulade Sauce II, page 110). Either version makes a delicious dressing for cold shrimp, so take your pick.

Serves 4

4 large and 4 small leaves butter lettuce
1 cup Rémoulade Sauce I or II (page 110)
20 medium or 16 large shrimp, steamed (left),
chilled, and peeled, tail shells left on

Line 4 small salad plates with the outer lettuce leaves. Place a small leaf in the center of each to serve as a cup and fill with the sauce. Surround with the shrimp.

Shrimp Rémoulade with Rémoulade Sauce II

Shrimp Toast

This Chinese-Vietnamese appetizer is usually deep-fried, but unless the bread is just the right degree of staleness and the oil temperature is just right, the bread can absorb a lot of oil and the final product can be unappetizingly greasy. Cooking shrimp toasts under the broiler produces an equally tasty result with less mess and fewer calories. Try them plain or wrapped in a tender lettuce leaf and drizzled with Nuoc Cham (see page 111).

Serves 6 to 8

> ½ *pound shrimp (any size), peeled and deveined*
> 1 *tablespoon minced fresh pork fat*
> 2 *green onions, white part only, chopped*
> 2 *tablespoons fresh mint, coriander, or basil leaves*
> 1 *teaspoon fish sauce (see Note, page 111)*
> ¼ *teaspoon kosher salt*
> *Pinch of white pepper*
> 24 *small or 16 large diagonal slices*
>   (½ *inch thick) sweet French bread*
> 12 *small or 8 medium shrimp, peeled,*
>   *split lengthwise, and deveined*

1. Combine the ½ pound shrimp, pork fat, green onions, and herbs in a food processor or blender and chop to a fine paste. (To make by hand, mince the ingredients together with a knife, chopping repeatedly until the mixture is smooth and fluffy.) Add the fish sauce, salt, and pepper and blend. Refrigerate until ready to use (may be made up to a day ahead).

2. Spread the bread slices on a baking sheet and toast them lightly on one side in a low oven; the bread should dry out slightly, but not brown. Let cool. Spread the untoasted sides with the shrimp mixture, spreading it all the way to the edges of the bread and mounding it slightly in the middle. Twist a shrimp half and lightly press it into the top of each toast.

3. Arrange the slices shrimp side up on a broiling pan, with the side showing more crust away from the heat if possible. Broil 3 to 4 inches from the heat until the topping is opaque and the bread is golden brown, about 5 minutes. Serve the toasts hot or warm, with lettuce leaves for wrapping and Nuoc Cham for dipping if desired.

Saté Udang
(Grilled Marinated Shrimp)

These spicy Indonesian-style grilled shrimp can be served as an appetizer in an Asian or Western meal. Or you can serve them as an entrée over plain rice. In either case, beer or a cold fruit drink is in order because the chile in the marinade packs a punch.

Serves 6 to 8

> *1 clove garlic*
> **Pinch of kosher salt**
> *1 small fresh green or red chile, minced* **OR**
> *¼ teaspoon Indonesian-style fresh chile paste*
>   *(sambal ulek)*
> **2 tablespoons soy sauce**
> **1 tablespoon lemon or lime juice**
> **1 teaspoon molasses**
> **1 pound medium or large shrimp, peeled and**
>   *deveined, tail shells left on*

1. Pound the garlic and salt to a paste in a mortar or with the side of a large knife blade. Transfer to a bowl, add the chile, soy sauce, lemon juice, and molasses, and stir to combine. Add the shrimp and marinate 30 minutes. If using bamboo or wooden skewers, soak them in water for 15 minutes before skewering to prevent them from burning on the grill.

2. Thread the shrimp on thin skewers, passing the skewer through the thick end from above, then back through the thin end. Skewer shrimp individually or several to a skewer. Grill over a hot fire on an open grill or broil 2 to 3 inches from the heat until the meat is opaque, 2 to 3 minutes per side. Baste with the marinade during and after cooking.

Variation Another method of skewering shrimp for grilling is shown in the photo opposite. Line up 2 or 3 shrimp and pass one skewer through all of them near the head end. Run another skewer through the tail ends.

Note The authentic Indonesian version of this marinade would call for *kecap manis,* a thick, sweetened and spiced soy sauce from Java. Regular soy sauce plus molasses makes a near substitute.

Shrimp and Fresh Corn Tamales

I love the flavor and color combination of shrimp and sweet yellow corn. Fresh corn tamales are popular all over Mexico, where they are made with the large-kerneled field corn that, in dried form, is the basis for hominy and tortillas. North American sweet corn varieties do not have the same starch content, however, so we have to add dried corn in the form of hominy grits to get a similar texture. When sweet corn is not in season, you may use frozen corn kernels and dried corn husks. The latter are sold in Mexican markets and by mail order through international foods catalogues.

Serves 6 to 8

> *½ cup lard or vegetable shortening*
> *1⅓ cups quick-cooking grits*
> *1½ teaspoons kosher salt*
> *½ cup lukewarm unsalted chicken stock*
> *4 large ears fresh sweet corn (2½ cups kernels)*
> *1 teaspoon baking powder*
> *2 large green poblano or Anaheim chiles,*
> *   roasted and peeled, seeds and ribs removed*
> *24 medium shrimp, peeled and deveined*

1. Beat the lard with an electric mixer until very light. Meanwhile, grind the grits as finely as possible in 2 or 3 batches in a blender or all at once in a food processor. Add the grits and salt to the beaten lard and beat until thoroughly blended. With the mixer running at medium-high speed, add the stock in a thin stream. Continue beating until the stock is all incorporated, stopping to scrape the bowl once or twice. Set aside to cool.

2. Cut through the ears of corn about ½ inch above the base. Carefully peel away the leaves, trying not to tear them. Remove the silk from the ears and cut off the kernels into a bowl. Do not cut too deeply; you want to get only the top two-thirds of each kernel. With the back of the knife, scrape the cut cobs to squeeze out the milky centers into the bowl. Measure 2½ cups of the cut corn.

3. Add the corn to the blender (in batches) or processor (all at once) with ½ cup water and blend to a rough puree. Add to the mixing bowl and beat until incorporated. Stir in the baking powder.

4. For steaming, you will need a steaming pot with a removable basket that can hold the tamales snugly above at least 2 inches of boiling water. Trim the tops of the corn leaves and blanch them if necessary to make them flexible. (The water in the steamer is fine for this purpose.) Drain them well and separate any leaves still stuck together. Tear the tough outermost leaves into ¼-inch strips to use for tying the tamales; use the smallest leaves to line the steamer basket. Cut the chiles into thin strips. Make a few shallow cuts in the inner curve of each shrimp to make them easier to straighten.

5. To assemble each tamale, spread a corn leaf out on the table. Spread 2 tablespoons of the corn mixture into a 3-inch square in the center of the leaf. Gently press a shrimp and a couple of chile strips into the dough lengthwise. Roll the leaf snugly around the filling and fold the wide end of the roll over the top. Tie with a strip of leaf (or use kitchen twine). Twist the tapered end closed and tie with another piece of leaf or twine. Continue with the remaining tamales. Lay the finished tamales in the steamer or stand them side by side, pointed ends up. Cover with more leaves and steam 2 hours. Keep the water in the steamer at a lively simmer, but do not boil too hard or it may boil dry before the tamales are done.

6. Remove the tamales from the steamer and serve hot or warm. Tamales may be eaten out of hand as a snack or, for a more formal presentation, serve them on a plate with a simple tomato sauce.

Serve Shrimp and Fresh Corn Tamales
as part of a buffet of Mexican appetizers.

Shrimp Smoked in the Shell

Hot-smoking, or smoke-cooking, is not a means of preserving foods, just another way of adding flavor. Shrimp may be smoked in a smoker, in a covered barbecue kettle, or Chinese-style—on top of the stove in a wok. Serve smoked shrimp in their shells, hot or at room temperature; peel at the table.

Serves 4 to 6

> *1 pound medium or large shrimp, deveined in the shell*

> **MARINADE**
> *¼ cup dry sherry or Chinese rice wine*
> *¼ cup water*
> *3 tablespoons soy sauce*
> *2 tablespoons minced fresh ginger*
> *1 teaspoon kosher salt*

> **FOR A SMOKER OR COVERED BARBECUE**
> *1 cup hardwood smoking chips (hickory, alder, or oak)*

> **FOR A WOK**
> *¼ cup raw rice*
> *¼ cup brown sugar*
> *¼ cup loose black or jasmine tea*

1. Combine the marinade ingredients and stir to dissolve the salt. Toss the shrimp in the marinade and let stand 30 minutes.

Smoker method

2. Smoke according to the manufacturer's instructions for uncooked shellfish. Some woods give a stronger smoke flavor than others, so you might want to experiment a bit with the amount and type of smoking chips to use to suit your taste.

Barbecue kettle method

2. Soak the smoking chips in a bowl with water to cover. Build a moderate charcoal fire off-center in a covered grill and let it burn until the coals are coated with gray ash, 30 to 45 minutes. Drain the shrimp and spread them out on a cake cooling rack, a piece of screen, or any wire surface that will keep the shrimp from slipping through the grill but allow the smoke to surround them. (If large enough, shrimp can be skewered as for Grilled Shrimp Brochettes, page 30, and placed directly on the grill surface.)

3. Drain the smoking chips and add them to the fire. Replace the grill and add the shrimp on their rack, on the opposite side from the fire. Cover and cook 15 minutes, or until the shrimp meat is opaque and the shells have taken on a smoky color.

Wok method

2. Line a large wok and its domed lid with enough heavy-duty aluminum foil to extend 1 inch beyond the edge of the lid. Combine the rice, sugar, and tea and scatter them over the bottom of the wok. Put the shrimp on a round rack above the rice mixture.

3. Place the wok over high heat. When the rice mixture begins to burn and release smoke, cover the wok, crimping the foil layers together to form a tight seal. Reduce the heat to medium and cook 9 minutes for medium shrimp, 10 minutes for large.

4. Open the wok under an exhaust fan or near an open window (to keep from smoking everything in the house), remove the shrimp, and wrap the foil tightly around the smoking mixture. Let the package cool, then dispose of it promptly.

Grilled Shrimp Brochettes with Dipping Sauces

Grilling shrimp in the shell intensifies their flavor like no other cooking method. Any size of raw shrimp, from 61-70s to under-10s (see page 11) and giant freshwater prawns, may be grilled, although the cooking time will vary according to size. Small shrimp may be eaten shell and all, but larger shrimp generally have to be peeled.

Serves 6 to 8

> 1½ *pounds unpeeled shrimp, any size*
> *Peanut oil*
> *Kosher salt*
> *Pepper*
> *Nuoc Cham (see page 111)*

1. If using bamboo or wooden skewers, soak them in water for 15 minutes before skewering to prevent them from burning on the grill. Rinse the shrimp and drain well. Devein through the shell if desired. To skewer a shrimp, pass a skewer through it near the head end, starting from the outer (dorsal) side and coming out through the legs on the inner (ventral) side. Then curl the shrimp into a crescent (the way it normally curls in cooking) and pass the skewer through near the tail end from the ventral to the dorsal side. Allow anywhere from 2 to 8 shrimp per skewer, depending on size. Arrange the shrimp brochettes in a shallow pan, drizzle with a little oil, and sprinkle with salt and pepper. Keep refrigerated until about 15 minutes before cooking.

2. Prepare a hot charcoal fire in a hibachi or other open grill, and preheat the grill surface thoroughly. Cook the shrimp over the hottest part of the fire until the shells are red and the meat is opaque white, 2 to 5 minutes per side depending on size. If you like a glossy appearance, brush the shells with the oil during cooking (it won't affect the flavor). Serve with Nuoc Cham, Thai Sweet and Sour Dipping Sauce (see page 111), or Soy-Ginger Dipping Sauce (see page 112).

Variation For a more sociable form of cooking and eating, skewer each shrimp individually near the end of a skewer. Invite your guests to cook their own on a hibachi or other small grill placed in the center of the table.

Variation You can also broil shrimp brochettes. Skewer and marinate as above. Position the broiler rack so the shrimp will be no more than 2 to 3 inches from the heat and cook 2 to 5 minutes per side, depending on size.

Camarones en Sangrita (Grilled Shrimp with Tequila and Pomegranate Marinade)

Sangrita is a popular Mexican cocktail, sometimes mixed with tequila but more authentically served alongside a shot of the fiery liquor. When made less sweet than is typical for drinking, it makes an intriguing marinade for grilled shrimp. Fresh pomegranate juice is more authentic, but grenadine syrup (made from pomegranates) is much more widely available. Serve these shrimp as an appetizer with chilled beer or margaritas.

Serves 4

> 1 pound medium or large shrimp,
>   deveined in the shell
> Lime wedges
>
> MARINADE
> ¼ cup lemon or lime juice
> 2 tablespoons grenadine syrup
> 2 ounces tequila
> ¾ teaspoon kosher salt
> ¼ to ½ teaspoon Tabasco or other liquid hot
>   pepper sauce

1. Combine the marinade ingredients in a bowl, add the shrimp, and marinate 30 minutes to 1 hour, turning occasionally. Do not marinate any longer or the lemon juice will "cook" the shrimp.

2. Drain the shrimp and skewer them as directed in Grilled Shrimp Brochettes with Dipping Sauces (see page 30). Grill over a medium to hot fire or broil 3 inches from the heat until the shells turn pink and the meat is opaque, 2 to 4 minutes per side. Serve with lime wedges.

Shrimp Ceviche with Mango

Ceviche, raw fish or shellfish "cooked" by steeping it in lime juice, is a popular treat all across the Pacific. The variations are endless; Latin American versions typically include tomato, while Southeast Asian and Polynesian versions are likely to be flavored with coconut milk. This version, native to no particular region, uses cubes of mango to help smooth the flavors of the lime juice and chile. Substitute papaya if you like.

Serves 4 to 6

> ½ pound medium shrimp, peeled, split lengthwise,
>   and deveined
> ¼ cup fresh lime or lemon juice
> 1 small green chile, seeds and ribs removed,
>   minced
> 2 tablespoons minced green or red onion
> 1 small mango, ripe but firm, peeled and diced
> Kosher salt to taste
> Fresh coriander (cilantro) or mint, for garnish

1. Place the shrimp in a small glass or stainless steel bowl and cover with lime juice. Cover and refrigerate 30 minutes to overnight (see Technique Note), stirring occasionally.

2. About 30 minutes before serving, stir in the remaining ingredients. Serve in stemmed glasses or as a salad on top of shredded lettuce. Garnish with coriander or mint sprigs.

Technique Note How long to steep the shrimp in lime is a matter of personal preference. A memorable ceviche I tasted in a Bangkok restaurant had been cured for just a few minutes and the shrimp was still virtually raw. It was perfectly delicious, but the texture might startle your guests. While testing these recipes, I put a bowl of marinating shrimp in the refrigerator and forgot about it. When I discovered it two weeks later, it was still edible, though just a bit tough. Somewhere between 1 hour and 24 hours of marinating is probably best.

Dancing Prawns

If you can find large shrimp with their heads still attached, try this unusual Thai dish. After being deveined through the shell, the shrimp are stuffed with a spiced pork mixture, which gives both richness and flavor to the shrimp meat. The recipe will also work with headless shrimp, but skewer them in the opposite direction (that is, from tail to head) so they "dance" with their tails in the air. After pulling the shrimp off the skewers, you can eat them with a knife and fork, but they are really easier to peel and eat with your fingers.

Serves 4 to 6

>   *2 ounces moderately fatty pork, ground or minced*
>   *1 small clove garlic, minced*
>   *1 tablespoon minced shallot*
>   *2 teaspoons minced lemongrass (see Note)*
>   *1 teaspoon minced fresh galingale (see Note,*
>   *page 48) or ginger*
>   *Pinch of kosher salt*
>   *1 tablespoon each lemon juice, soy sauce, and*
>   *Chinese rice wine or dry sherry*
>   *12 large or jumbo shrimp, preferably whole*
>   *½ orange or apple*
>   *Coriander (cilantro) sprigs, for garnish*
>   *Lime wedges*

1. Mince the pork as finely as possible with a knife, and place it in a small bowl. In a mortar, pound the garlic, shallot, lemongrass, and galingale to a paste with a pinch of salt. Add it to the pork and stir in the lemon juice, soy sauce, and wine. Beat or knead the mixture to a smooth consistency. To make the stuffing in a food processor, simply combine the preceding ingredients in the processor and chop to a paste.

2. Soak a dozen 8-inch or longer bamboo skewers in water for at least 15 minutes (to keep them from burning) while you prepare the shrimp. Devein the shrimp through the shell (see page 16), making a deeper cut than usual, as if butterflying the shrimp. Straighten out a single shrimp and thread it lengthwise on a skewer, starting in the mouth, passing through the head and abdomen, and coming out through the tail. (Watch out for the sharp rostrum projecting from the top of the head.) Push the skewer on through until just a bit of the blunt end extends from the mouth. Spread the shell and meat apart slightly and stuff the opening with about a teaspoonful of the pork mixture, packing it in well and smoothing over the surface. Repeat with the remaining shrimp.

3. Handling the skewers by the pointed ends, grill the shrimp over a medium-hot fire (or cook under a broiler) until the meat is opaque, about 3 minutes per side. To serve, place the orange or apple cut side down on a plate and insert the pointed ends of the skewers. Garnish with coriander sprigs and lime wedges. Serve with Thai Sweet and Sour Dipping Sauce (see page 111), Nuoc Cham (page 111), or Soy-Ginger Dipping Sauce (page 112) with a little hot pepper sauce added.

Variation You can use the same stuffing for 6 to 8 jumbo freshwater prawns. Skewer them as directed above, but remove them from the skewers after cooking and serve on a plate—they are too big to try to balance in the "dancing" position.

Note Fresh lemongrass is available in some Asian markets; it's being grown commercially in California and on the Gulf Coast. It comes in the form of stiff, waxy stalks and has a distinctive citrus-blossom flavor and aroma. Only the bottom third of the stalk is tender enough to be eaten, and that must be sliced crosswise and very finely minced or ground to a paste. If you can't find fresh lemongrass, look for dried flakes in herb shops (they're used in herbal teas); they can be minced after soaking briefly in water. Otherwise, substitute a teaspoon of grated lemon or lime zest.

Shrimp in Beer

These quick-pickled shrimp are easy to make and ideal to have on hand in the refrigerator for drop-in guests or instant snacks. Although I generally make them when I have excess shrimp, say from buying a box of frozen shrimp, it's definitely worth buying shrimp just for this recipe. Feel free to vary the seasonings; dill or caraway seeds are appropriate additions. And because the beer provides a lot of the flavor, use a good one, such as a top-quality Danish or German lager.

Serves 8

> *¾ pound medium shrimp, deveined in the shell and steamed (see page 20)*
> *1 lemon, thinly sliced*
> *2 whole dried red chiles OR ¼ teaspoon red pepper flakes*
> *8 peppercorns, cracked*
> *4 cloves*
> *½ teaspoon kosher salt*
> *1 bottle (12 ounces) flat beer*
> *2 small cloves garlic, peeled*

1. Pack the shrimp and lemon slices into two 1-pint mason jars, alternating layers of shrimp and lemon. Divide the chiles, pepper, cloves, and salt evenly between the jars. Bring the beer and garlic to a boil in a non-aluminum saucepan and cook just until any foam disappears. Pour the beer over the shrimp to cover, and put a clove of garlic in each jar. Seal the jars immediately, let cool, and refrigerate 24 hours to 2 weeks.

2. To serve, drain the shrimp well. (Reserve the pickling liquid in case there are any leftovers, which is unlikely.) Serve plain in a bowl, or dress them up a bit by arranging them on lettuce leaves. No sauce is really needed, but if you like, dip them in Rémoulade Sauce I or II or Cocktail Sauce (see page 110).

Technique Note It's important to use flat beer for the pickling liquid, or it will foam like crazy when boiled and produce a lot of bubbles in the jar, which may affect the seal.

Chesapeake Bay Steamed Shrimp

"Steaming" is a favorite cooking method for shrimp and crab in the Chesapeake Bay region. There the shellfish may be either cooked over steam or boiled in a small amount of water in a covered pot. I prefer the former method, which uses a pot with a removable steaming insert or a free-standing steamer rack inside a large saucepan. Some supermarkets and fish markets sell very good Chesapeake Bay–style seafood seasoning mixes. You can use one or make your own with a spice grinder. Don't be alarmed by the amount of seasoning called for; most of it is left clinging to the shells.

Serves 4 to 6

> 1½ pounds whole OR 1 pound headless shrimp,
>   medium or larger
> Water
> Distilled or cider vinegar
> 2 tablespoons Chesapeake seafood seasoning
>   (packaged or homemade)
> 1 to 2 teaspoons kosher salt or to taste

CHESAPEAKE SEAFOOD SEASONING
2 teaspoons kosher salt
2 tablespoons celery seed
2 teaspoons each peppercorns and mustard seed
4 bay leaves
6 cloves
¼ teaspoon ground ginger
½ teaspoon mace flakes OR ¼ teaspoon ground
½ cinnamon stick
1 teaspoon paprika
¼ teaspoon cayenne pepper, more or less to taste
¼ teaspoon cardamom seed (about 2 pods)

1. If you want to make your own Chesapeake seafood seasoning, combine the seasoning ingredients in a spice grinder and grind to a coarse powder. You will get about ⅓ cup. Store in a tightly sealed jar.

2. Devein the shrimp through the shells, if desired. Fill the steaming pot to a depth of at least 1 inch with 4 parts water to 1 part vinegar; the liquid should not rise above the bottom of the steaming rack. Combine the seasoning mix and salt. Place the shrimp in the steamer in layers, sprinkling each layer heavily with seasoning mix. Bring to a boil, cover, and steam until the shrimp meat is opaque white, 5 to 10 minutes depending on size. Transfer the shrimp to a serving bowl to be peeled at the table. Serve with beer.

Vietnamese Triangle Spring Rolls

All over East Asia thin dough wrapped around a savory filling and deep-fried until crisp is a favorite snack. Chinese "egg rolls" and Philippine *lumpia* are perhaps better known, but to my taste the Vietnamese spring rolls (*cha gio*) in their transparent rice-paper wrappers are the most delicious example of the genre. In this variation on spring rolls, whole butterflied shrimp form the backbones of the rolls, while their tail shells serve as convenient handles for dipping in a sauce. They are equally at home with an Asian meal or Western cocktails.

Rice papers (*banh trang*) are translucent, brittle sheets made by drying a rice-flour paste on mats of woven bamboo. A specialty of Vietnam, they are now imported from Thailand and are available wherever there is a Vietnamese community, including most Chinatowns. They come in various shapes, including large and small rounds and quarter-rounds, but 9-inch rounds are the most common.

Serves 6 to 8

24 medium shrimp
1 tablespoon oil
1 tablespoon each *minced ginger and garlic*
¼ pound minced pork or ground beef
3 green onions, finely sliced (½ cup)
Kosher salt and pepper to taste
1 cup bean sprouts, blanched and cut into
  1-inch lengths
¼ cup mint leaves, chopped
8 9-inch round sheets rice paper
1 egg white, lightly beaten
Oil for deep-frying

1. Butterfly 16 of the shrimp, leaving the tail shells attached. Peel, devein, and chop the remaining shrimp. Heat the tablespoon of oil in a skillet over low heat and cook the ginger and garlic until fragrant. Add the minced pork and green onions and cook until the meat loses its raw color. Stir in the chopped shrimp and cook until it turns pink. Season to taste with salt and pepper. Let cool, then stir in the bean sprouts and mint.

2. Bend the rice papers against a straight edge to break them in half. Moisten 2 large clean kitchen towels and wring out the excess water. Lay a towel out on the table and spread a single layer of rice papers over half the towel. Fold the towel over and add another layer of rice papers. Top these with another towel and continue until all the rice papers are between layers of towel. (You may need a third towel.) Turn over the stack and let it stand until the rice papers are soft and pliable, about 10 minutes.

→

3. Peel away the towel to expose the top layer of rice papers, but leave them on the towel. Brush a piece of rice paper lightly with egg white. Spread a shrimp out flat near one corner, with the tail extending just past the straight edge (see illustration). Place 1½ teaspoons of the stuffing in a neat pile on the shrimp. Fold the triangle of shrimp, stuffing, and paper over toward the center of the sheet; the tail will now be perpendicular to the straight edge. Fold the triangle over again, so the first fold lines up with the straight edge. Lifting by the tail, fold the triangle over the opposite side to match the far edge of the semicircle. Fold the two remaining flaps over the triangle. Repeat with the remaining papers and stuffing. Transfer the rolls to a sheet pan and refrigerate, covered with a damp towel, until ready to cook.

4. Heat the frying oil (at least 1½ inches deep) to 350° in a wok or deep skillet. Fry the rolls a few at a time until the skins are browned and transparent, about 3 minutes. Drain on paper towels and serve with Nuoc Cham (see page 111) or Soy-Ginger Dipping Sauce (page 112). *Caution:* Even with careful folding, the rice paper does not always provide a perfect seal, and hot oil can leak into the packages. It's best to bite off a corner of the roll first, then let any liquid from inside the roll drip out before eating the rest.

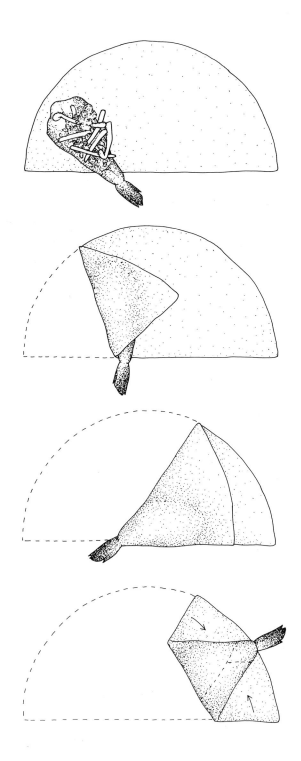

Mixed Seafood Terrine (page 44)

Mixed Seafood Terrine

A terrine is like a pâté, but it is not baked in a crust. Terrines are often multilayered affairs, with alternating tiers of different colors and flavors. This one is relatively simple, with orange-pink shrimp and light green leeks peeking out between layers of a pale fish and shellfish puree.

Serves 10 to 12

> 1 bunch (about 1½ pounds) leeks
> 2 tablespoons fresh tarragon leaves
> ¼ cup fresh chervil or curly parsley leaves
> 1 cup finely shredded sorrel leaves (about 12
>   small leaves)
> 1 teaspoon unsalted butter or oil
> ½ pound fillet of firm, lean fish such as halibut,
>   sole, or monkfish, well chilled
> ½ pound fillet of richer fish such as salmon,
>   Greenland turbot, or sablefish (see Note),
>   well chilled
> ¼ pound scallops, well chilled (optional)
> ¾ pound medium or large shrimp, peeled
>   and deveined, well chilled
> 1¼ teaspoons kosher salt
> ⅛ teaspoon white pepper
> 3 large egg whites
> 1 cup cold whipping cream

1. Cut off the green tops from the leeks and reserve. (The cut tops should be 10 to 12 inches long.) Cut 1 cup of slices from the white parts; reserve the rest for another use. Wash the tops well, discarding any yellowed or beat-up leaves. Split the tops lengthwise and separate the leaves. Parboil until soft, about 10 minutes, drain, cover with cold water, and set aside.

2. Blanch the herbs separately just until wilted. (An easy way to do this is to place them in a sieve and lower it into a pot of simmering water.) Rinse with cold water and drain. The sorrel will take longer than the others. Don't be alarmed when it turns a sickly olive green a few seconds after it hits the water; the color will come back somewhat later. Sauté the sliced leeks in butter until soft; set aside to cool.

3. Cut the fish into 1-inch cubes and place them in a food processor with the scallops and one-third of the shrimp. If using a blender, you will have to grind the mixture in several batches. Add the herbs, salt, and pepper and process to a smooth paste. Transfer the mixture to a bowl and return to the refrigerator while you prepare the pan.

4. Butter a standard loaf pan or coat it with vegetable cooking spray. Cut the leek leaves to about 8 inches in length and slit them open lengthwise. Carefully separate the two sides of each leaf, exposing the inner pulp (this is easiest to do with the leaves still in the water). Line the bottom and sides of the pan with the flattened leaves, draping the excess over the sides of the pan. Preheat the oven to 375° and have ready a kettle of hot water and a baking dish big enough to hold the loaf pan. Butterfly the remaining shrimp and give them a smack with the side of a broad-bladed knife to flatten them slightly.

5. Return the seafood mixture to the processor and add the egg whites. With the motor running, add the cream through the feed tube. Process to a smooth, slightly wet paste. Drop a quarter of the mixture by spoonfuls into the loaf pan and gently spread it over the bottom, being careful not to dislodge the leaves. Arrange half the shrimp over the top in a single layer, coming not quite to the edges. Top with another quarter of the seafood mixture. Spread the sliced leeks in an even layer over the top. Add another layer of the seafood mixture, another layer of shrimp, and the rest of the seafood mixture. Lift the pan a couple of inches off the table and drop it two or three times to knock out

any large air pockets. Fold the loose ends of the leaves over the top and cover the top with more leaves running lengthwise.

6. Place the loaf pan inside the baking dish, place them in the oven, and carefully add enough hot water to the baking dish to come at least halfway up the sides of the loaf pan. Bake until the mixture is firm and the center reads 140° on a meat thermometer, about 40 to 50 minutes. Chill in the pan, unmold, and serve in ½-inch slices. The leek wrapping is edible and should be served along with the slices. If a sauce is desired, spoon a lightly cooked and seasoned fresh tomato sauce onto each plate first, then top with a slice of terrine.

Note Using some higher-fat fish in the blend makes for a richer, moister terrine. Salmon gives a nice flavor and texture, but it does add a pink color that reduces the contrast with the shrimp layer. Greenland turbot, actually a type of halibut, is nearly as rich as salmon, but white and mild in flavor, as is sablefish, a north Pacific fish also known as black cod or butterfish. Avoid darker fish such as mackerel or tuna because they would overwhelm the flavor of the other seafoods.

Technique Note For a light-textured terrine, it's important that the seafood mixture be quite cold when blending in the cream. On a warm day, put the fish in the freezer for a half hour or so before blending.

Shrimp Cocktail

Shrimp cocktail is one of the most popular appetizers in restaurants coast to coast. I don't have any figures to back this up, but I would guess that Americans eat more shrimp in the form of shrimp cocktails than in any other form, with the possible exception of battered and fried.

Serves 4

> *4 red-leaf or butter lettuce leaves*
> *1 cup shredded lettuce*
> *½ cup Cocktail Sauce (see page 110)*
> *16 large shrimp, steamed (see page 20),*
>   *chilled, and peeled, tail shells left on*
> *4 lemon wedges*

Line 4 shallow stemmed glasses (champagne or oversized margarita glasses are traditional) with lettuce leaves, tearing each leaf open at the stem end and overlapping the lower parts to make the leaf as nearly circular as possible. Pile shredded lettuce in the center of each glass and top with Cocktail Sauce. Hang 4 shrimp around the edge of each glass. Notch the lemon wedges and fix 1 to the edge of each glass.

Variation You can also present Shrimp Rémoulade (see page 20) this way.

First Courses

Shrimp Cakes

Tom Yam Kung
(Thai Hot and Sour
Shrimp Soup)

In Thailand, as in other tropical regions, nearly every meal includes a piping hot soup, often liberally laced with chiles. The temperature and the chiles combine to induce cooling perspiration. If you have access to a well-stocked Asian market, you should be able to find the ingredients that give this soup its special flavor—lemongrass, dried citrus leaves, fresh coriander (cilantro) with the roots still attached, and the exotic ginger relative called galingale or *kha* (see Note). These and other Southeast Asian specialties are also available in dried form by mail from DeWildt Imports, Inc., RD 3, Bangor, PA 18013 (free catalogue on request; phone 215–588–4949).

Serves 4 to 6

> *1 tablespoon oil*
> *¾ pound medium or large shrimp, peeled and*
>   *deveined, shells reserved*
> *1 stalk fresh lemongrass, thinly sliced*
>   *OR 1 tablespoon dried lemongrass leaves*
> *3 slices fresh or dried galingale (see Note)*
>   *OR ¼ teaspoon turmeric*
> *5–6 fresh coriander (cilantro) stems*
>   *(include roots, if attached)*
> *½ teaspoon peppercorns, cracked*
> *1 or 2 small fresh chiles, roughly chopped*
> *2 dried lime leaves (optional)*
> *1½ quarts water or chicken stock*
> *2 green onions, sliced*
> *Juice of 1 lime*
> *1 teaspoon kosher salt*
> *1 cup sliced mushrooms (optional)*
> *Fish sauce to taste (see Note, page 111)*
> *Coriander leaves, for garnish*
> *1 fresh red or green chile, sliced, loose seeds*
>   *removed, for garnish*

1. Heat the oil in a wok or saucepan over low heat. Add the shrimp shells, lemongrass, galingale, coriander stems, peppercorns, chopped chiles, and lime leaves, and cook until the shrimp shells turn red. (Optional: if using fresh lemongrass, save 1 tablespoon of very thin slices from the bottom of the stalk to add to the soup in step 2.) Add the water or stock and simmer 15 minutes.

2. Strain the stock and return it to the pan. Add the shrimp, green onions, lime juice, salt, mushrooms, and lemongrass slices (if used), and simmer until the shrimp turn pink and opaque. Season to taste with fish sauce, and garnish with coriander leaves and sliced chiles.

Variation For a more substantial soup, soak 1 ounce of transparent bean thread noodles in hot water until soft. (These noodles, also known as Chinese vermicelli or cellophane noodles, are available in Chinese markets.) Drain and add to the soup along with the shrimp.

Note Galingale (*kha*), sometimes spelled galangal or galanga, is a relative of ginger, but its distinctive mustardy aroma is more like that of turmeric. It is being grown now in Fiji and Hawaii, and you may find it fresh in Southeast Asian markets. Otherwise, look for it in dried slices in plastic bags. A teaspoonful of the ground form, also known as laos powder, is a distant third choice. If none of these is available, use turmeric—it will stain the soup yellow, but the flavor will be similar.

If you can find galingale, chances are you can find the dried leaves of the kaffir lime tree. Better still, if you have access to an unsprayed citrus tree, use its leaves, fresh or dried.

Coconut and Tamarind Shrimp Salad

Serve this rather wet salad in small bowls as a first course or alongside other dishes as a refreshing counterpoint to spicier foods.

Serves 4

> 2 ounces block tamarind (see Note, page 84)
> 2 tablespoons vegetable oil
> 2 tablespoons minced garlic
> 2 tablespoons minced ginger
> Seeds from 1 cardamom pod (⅛ teaspoon)
> 3 or 4 small red chiles, seeded and cut into
>   thin strips
> 2 tablespoons fish sauce (see Note, page 111)
> ½ pound small or medium shrimp, peeled and
>   deveined (split medium shrimp in half
>   lengthwise)
> ¼ cup basil leaves (or equal parts basil and mint),
>   shredded
> 1 cup grated fresh coconut
> Basil leaves and blossoms, for garnish

1. Place the tamarind pulp in a small bowl and cover it with 1 cup hot water. Soak until thoroughly softened, then strain, pushing as much of the pulp as possible through the sieve. Discard the strings and seeds.

2. Heat the oil in a wok or skillet over moderate heat. Add the garlic, ginger, cardamom, and chile strips and cook until fragrant but not browned. Add the strained tamarind water and fish sauce, bring to a boil, and reduce to a simmer. Add the shrimp and simmer until just cooked, about 3 to 5 minutes. Transfer the shrimp and sauce to a bowl and chill. When cold, add the shredded basil and coconut, taste for seasoning, and chill until ready to serve. Garnish with additional basil leaves and blossoms.

Technique Note To get at the meat of a fresh coconut, hold it in one hand and tap it sharply with a hammer until it cracks. Or put it on a baking sheet in a 450° oven and bake until it cracks. Pour out the clear liquid and pry the shell open with a clean screwdriver or oyster knife. Pry the meat loose from the shell and grate it on a box grater.

Coconut and Tamarind Shrimp Salad

Shrimp Louis

Shrimp or crab salad with a tomato-flavored Louis dressing has been a California favorite since before the turn of the century. Although mayonnaise-based dressings are the rule today, the original was closer to a vinaigrette, flavored with bottled chili sauce and Worcestershire sauce. Mayonnaise was added somewhat later, probably to keep the dressing from separating. Here is a mayonnaise-less version.

Serves 2

> 1 head green or red-leaf lettuce
>   or an assortment of leaf lettuces
> 1 cup (about ⅓ pound) tiny cooked and
>   peeled shrimp
> 2 hard-boiled eggs, sliced or quartered
> Cooked fresh asparagus spears (if in season)
> Cherry tomatoes or tomato wedges (if in season)
>
> **LOUIS DRESSING**
> 2 tablespoons chili sauce
> 1 tablespoon Dijon-style mustard
> 1 tablespoon fresh lemon juice
> Dash of Worcestershire sauce
> ½ cup mild olive oil or other salad oil
> 1 tablespoon chopped chives

1. Prepare the dressing as follows: Combine the chili sauce, mustard, lemon juice, and Worcestershire sauce in a bowl and whisk together. Add the oil gradually, whisking constantly. Stir in the chives and refrigerate at least 1 hour.

2. Line 2 dinner plates or shallow salad bowls with outer lettuce leaves; tear the remaining leaves and arrange on top. Pile the shrimp in the center and arrange the eggs and asparagus or tomatoes around the sides. Stir the dressing and spoon ¼ cup on each salad; serve the remaining dressing on the side.

Shrimp and Orange Salad

A favorite salad of French-inspired California cooks combines tender curly endive and sweet oranges. Thai shrimp salads often mix cooked shrimp with assorted fruits and bits of fried shallot and garlic. I interwove those two threads and produced this salad. In an Asian meal it would be served not as a separate course but alongside other dishes, to be tasted as a refreshing interlude between bites of other, hotter foods.

Serves 4

> 2 tablespoons oil
> 2 cloves garlic, sliced
> 1 tablespoon sliced shallots
> ⅓ pound small or medium shrimp, steamed
>   (see page 20), peeled, and deveined
> 2 sweet oranges, peeled with a knife and
>   cut apart into sections
> 2 cups young, tender curly endive leaves
>   (preferably the smaller French variety
>   known as frisée)
> 1 small red or green chile, seeded and cut
>   into slivers
> 2 tablespoons lime juice
> Pinch of sugar
> Kosher salt to taste
> 1 red chile, for garnish (optional)

1. Heat the oil in a small skillet over low heat. Gently fry the garlic and shallots until golden brown and crisp. Do not cook too fast or they will become dark brown and bitter. Drain through a fine sieve, reserving the oil. Dry the fried pieces on a paper towel.

2. Arrange the shrimp and orange sections on a bed of endive leaves. Scatter the chile strips over all. Combine the lime juice, reserved garlic oil, sugar, and salt to taste. Drizzle the dressing over the salad and garnish with the fried garlic and shallot bits. Add a red chile cut into a blossom shape for garnish, if desired.

Shrimp Bisque

Shellfish bisques are part of the classic French restaurant repertoire, but they are not difficult to make at home if you have a food processor. This thick, highly seasoned soup is suffused with flavor that otherwise would be thrown away with the shrimp shells. It is best to use head-on shrimp because the fat inside the heads contributes both richness and flavor. The soup base (steps 1 through 4) may be made ahead of time and refrigerated overnight or frozen for longer storage.

Serves 6 to 8

> 1½ pounds head-on shrimp OR 1 pound headless
>   shrimp plus additional shells
> 3 tablespoons unsalted butter
> 1 carrot, finely diced
> 1 stalk celery, finely diced
> 1 small onion, finely diced
> ½ cup uncooked rice
> 1 ounce brandy
> 1 teaspoon kosher salt
> ½ teaspoon paprika
> Large pinch of cayenne pepper
> 3 sprigs parsley
> 1 sprig fresh thyme OR ½ teaspoon dried
> 1 bay leaf
> 2 cups milk or half-and-half
> Chopped chives, for garnish

> **COURT BOUILLON**
> 3½ cups water
> 1 cup dry white wine
> 3 or 4 sprigs parsley
> 1 onion, sliced
> 12 peppercorns

1. Combine the *court bouillon* ingredients in a non-aluminum saucepan. Bring just to a boil, reduce the heat, and simmer 30 minutes. Add the shrimp and simmer until the shells are bright red and the meat is opaque, about 10 minutes. Drain, reserving the broth. When the shrimp are cool enough to handle, peel and devein, reserving the heads and shells. Discard the onion and parsley; return broth to the pan.

2. Melt the butter in a large, heavy casserole or Dutch oven and cook the diced vegetables gently in it until they begin to soften. Meanwhile, add the rice to the broth and simmer uncovered.

3. Add the shrimp shells and heads to the vegetables in the large casserole, turn the heat to medium-high, and cook 5 minutes, stirring frequently. Regulate the heat to avoid scorching the butter. Add the brandy, let it come to a boil, and set it aflame with a long match. When the flames disappear, add the salt, paprika, cayenne pepper, broth, and rice. Tie the parsley, thyme, and bay leaf together with kitchen twine, or enclose them in cheesecloth, and add them to the soup. Cover and simmer 30 minutes or until the rice is very soft.

4. Add half the reserved shrimp meat to the soup and discard the herb bouquet. With a slotted spoon, transfer a quarter of the contents of the soup pot to a food processor (shells, meat, vegetables, and all) and grind to a puree, adding a little soup if necessary to facilitate blending. Strain the mixture through a fine sieve into a large bowl, pushing through as much of the puree as possible with a wooden spoon. Repeat until all the soup is blended and strained. Discard the shells.

5. Dice the remaining shrimp meat finely. Return the soup to the pot, add the milk and shrimp meat, and reheat gently. Adjust the seasoning if necessary. For the best flavor, hold the soup at serving temperature for 30 minutes or so before serving, but do not let it boil or the milk may curdle. Garnish with chives.

Jambalaya

In traditional Louisiana cookery, jambalaya is served as a first course or side dish. But, like the Spanish *paella* to which it is clearly related, it is substantial enough to be the centerpiece of a meal. To be authentic, jambalaya should include cubes of ham—the name is derived from the French word for ham, *jambon*. Most versions include shrimp. Other cooked meats, such as poached chicken or smoked sausage, can be added at the same time as the ham.

Serves 8

> ½ *pound medium shrimp, peeled and deveined, shells reserved*
> 2 *cups unsalted chicken stock*
> 1½ *tablespoons oil*
> 1 *cup each finely diced onion, celery, and green bell pepper*
> 1 *tablespoon minced garlic*
> ½ *teaspoon kosher salt*
> ½ *teaspoon each black and white pepper*
> ⅛ *to* ¼ *teaspoon cayenne pepper, according to taste*
> ½ *teaspoon dried thyme leaves, crushed*
> 2 *bay leaves*
> 2 *cups peeled, seeded, and chopped tomato OR 1 can (16 ounces) peeled tomatoes, drained and chopped*
> 4 *ounces good smoked ham, diced*
> 2 *cups raw long-grain unconverted rice*

1. Combine the shrimp shells and stock in a saucepan and add water to cover. Simmer 30 minutes uncovered, strain, and discard the shells. Add enough water to the strained stock to make 4 cups.

2. Heat the oil in a large, heavy pot and add the diced vegetables and garlic. Cook over medium heat, stirring frequently, until the onions are soft but not browned. Stir in the salt, peppers, thyme, and bay leaves and cook until fragrant. Add the tomatoes, ham, and stock and simmer 10 minutes. Taste for seasoning and adjust if necessary. (The sauce should be quite spicy; the rice will absorb a lot of the flavor.)

3. Stir in the rice and shrimp. Bring to a boil, reduce the heat, and simmer uncovered until the liquid drops to the level of the rice, about 15 minutes. Cover and cook over very low heat until all the liquid is absorbed and the rice is tender, 20 to 25 minutes. Remove the bay leaves before serving.

Variation Rock shrimp work especially well in this dish. Because they come already peeled, either use reserved shrimp shells to flavor the stock in step 1, or skip that step and just combine the stock and water—the flavor won't suffer much.

Shrimp, Okra, and Green Chile Gumbo

Although a lot of people associate gumbo only with Louisiana cookery, countless variations on the theme are found from Georgia to eastern Texas. This version reaches farther west to include large green chiles from New Mexico in place of the more typical bell peppers and cayenne pepper. They may not be traditional, but I like the flavor they give to a gumbo.

Serves 6 to 8

>   1 tablespoon kosher salt (less if using
>   canned stock)
>   ½ teaspoon each black and white pepper
>   1 teaspoon paprika
>   ½ teaspoon dried thyme
>   1 bay leaf, crumbled
>   3 green poblano chiles OR 4 or 5 green
>   Anaheim chiles, diced
>   1½ cups diced onion
>   1 cup diced celery
>   ½ cup peanut or corn oil
>   ⅔ cup all-purpose flour
>   1 pound fresh or frozen okra, stems removed,
>   sliced ½ inch thick
>   2 quarts unsalted chicken stock or Quick Shrimp
>   Stock (page 113)
>   1 pound medium or large shrimp, peeled
>   and deveined
>   Hot pepper sauce to taste
>   2 cups cooked long-grain rice

1. Combine the salt, pepper, paprika, thyme, and bay leaf in a small bowl and set aside. Combine the chiles, onion, and celery in another bowl and set aside.

2. In a heavy skillet, heat the oil over medium heat until a bit of flour foams on contact. Add the rest of the flour and cook slowly, stirring constantly, until the resulting roux is dark reddish-brown, 10 to 15 minutes. Lower the heat if necessary to prevent scorching.

3. Remove the pan from the heat and carefully add the diced chiles, onion, and celery. *Caution:* Don't let the roux spatter on your skin; it can cause severe burns. Stir to coat the vegetables with roux and return to medium-low heat. When the onion begins to soften, add half the okra and the mixed seasonings. Stir and cook 5 minutes, then remove from the heat.

4. Bring the stock to a boil in a large kettle. Add the vegetable and roux mixture and simmer until slightly thickened. Add the shrimp and the remaining okra and simmer 15 minutes more. Taste for seasoning and adjust if necessary with salt and liquid hot pepper sauce. Serve in bowls over rice.

Variation Feel free to add other shellfish in place of or in addition to the shrimp. Cooked crabmeat (in or out of the shell) and shucked oysters with their liquor are especially appropriate. You could also use cubes of firm fish, cooked chicken, smoked sausage, or ham. . . . The possibilities are endless.

Technique Note If you have never made a Louisiana-style roux before (step 2), allow plenty of time and be sure to have everything else ready so that you can give it your full attention. Stirring the roux as it cooks is essential to prevent it from scorching and turning bitter. As you gain experience, you will be able to keep one eye on the roux while you make other preparations, stopping to stir just often enough to keep the roux from scorching.

Ravioli with Shrimp Stuffing

This is an especially pretty dish: a pale pink shrimp stuffing fills pillows of spinach pasta, which are moistened with butter and broth, and garnished with bits of tomato. Roll out your own fresh pasta dough by hand or by machine, or buy uncut sheets of spinach dough from a delicatessen. (You will need about ⅔ pound.)

Asking for an ounce and a half of sole might get you laughed out of the fish market, so buy a little extra next time you cook fish and freeze the trimmings. This recipe makes more dough and filling than are needed for six servings, but it is not practical to make smaller quantities. Freeze any leftover ravioli on a cookie sheet, then transfer them to a tightly sealed package.

Serves 6

> *Spinach Noodle Dough (see page 60)*
> *3 large outer leaves of Savoy cabbage or*
> *   Chinese celery cabbage*
> *1 tablespoon oil*
> *½ cup diced onion*
> *1½ ounces fillet of sole, flounder, halibut,*
> *   or other mild white fish*
> *⅓ pound shrimp, peeled and deveined*
> *¼ teaspoon kosher salt*
> *Pinch of white pepper*
> *1 cup well-seasoned chicken stock*
> *¼ cup unsalted butter*
> *½ cup peeled and seeded tomatoes, finely diced*

1. Prepare the Spinach Noodle Dough through step 2 and let it rest while you prepare the filling.

2. Blanch or steam the cabbage leaves just until they wilt; remove them, keeping the hot water on the stove. Cool the cabbage leaves immediately in cold water, drain them, and chop them finely.

3. Heat the oil in a skillet and sauté the onion gently until soft. Add the cabbage and cook until nearly dry. Let cool.

4. Combine the fish and half the shrimp in a food processor or blender. Add the contents of the skillet and the salt and pepper; process to a smooth paste. Dice the remaining shrimp by hand into ¼-inch pieces and add them to the processor; combine with a few quick pulses, not enough to further chop the shrimp. Bring the pan of water back to a simmer and drop a small ball of the mixture in to cook. Taste it and adjust the seasonings as necessary.

5. Roll out a quarter of the pasta dough to about $\frac{1}{16}$ inch thick, the second thinnest setting on most pasta machines. Keep the rest of the dough covered. As you roll out the dough, make sure the sheet spreads to the full width of the rollers. Cut the ends of the finished sheet square and trim it to manageable lengths. (About 12 inches is plenty to handle at once.) If rolling out the dough by hand, cut the rolled sheet into 6- by 12-inch sections.

6. Place 1 tablespoon of the shrimp mixture every 3 inches along the length of the dough, about an inch in from the edge. Lightly moisten the dough along the edge and between the piles of filling with a pastry brush dipped in water. Fold the dough in half lengthwise, covering the filling and lining up the edges exactly; expel any air. Cut the dough into filled squares and crimp the cut edges with a fork, or use a special pastry wheel which cuts and crimps with one motion. Place the finished ravioli on a floured baking sheet and cover them with a towel. Repeat steps 5 and 6 until you have 18 ravioli.

7. Boil the ravioli (3 per serving) in salted water until the skin is tender and the filling has become firm, about 3 minutes after the water returns to a boil. Meanwhile, heat the stock, butter, and tomatoes in a large skillet. Drain the cooked ravioli, toss them in the skillet to moisten them with the sauce, and arrange them on warm plates. Spoon the sauce over the top.

Spinach Noodle Dough

Several of the pasta dishes in this chapter call for freshly made pasta. Here are recipes for the two most important fresh pasta doughs, egg and spinach. A pasta machine (the type with rollers, not the extruding type) makes short work of rolling out the dough to the desired thickness and cutting it into noodles, and most come with good directions. Most machines have cutters for two widths of noodle, ⅟₁₆ inch wide for the long, thin *tagliarini* and ¼ inch wide for *tagliatelle*. To my mind, the ideal noodle for seafood dishes is about ⅛ inch wide, the size of Genovese *trenette* or Roman *fettuccine*. The only way to get this cut is to cut it by hand. Stack the sheets of dough and roll them up like a jelly roll, then cut through the roll every ⅛ inch. Uncoil the noodles immediately after cutting or they may stick together.

Look for detailed instructions for making your own fresh pasta in most comprehensive Italian cookbooks; I particularly recommend *The Classic Italian Cookbook* and *More Classic Italian Cooking* by Marcella Hazan (Knopf) and *Bugialli on Pasta* by Giuliano Bugialli (Simon and Schuster).

Not all pasta dishes are automatically better with fresh pasta. Factory-made dried pasta, especially the imported Italian brands, is an excellent product and is more appropriate than fresh pasta in southern Italian dishes such as Spaghettini with Shrimp and Broccoli (see page 62).

Makes ¾ pound

> *Leaves and tender stems from 1 small (½-pound) bunch fresh spinach, washed*
> *1 large egg*
> *⅔ cup semolina (finely ground durum wheat flour, available in Italian delicatessens and health food stores)*
> *1 cup (approximately) all-purpose flour*

1. Blanch or steam the spinach until tender; rinse with cold water to stop the cooking and drain thoroughly.

2. *With a food processor:* Combine the spinach, egg, and semolina in the work bowl and process with the steel blade until the spinach is finely chopped. Add ⅔ cup flour and work the dough until it forms a ball. Let the machine run another 15 seconds to knead the dough. Turn the dough out onto a floured board and knead it a few times by hand, adding additional flour if necessary to make a smooth, slightly sticky dough. Cover with a bowl and let rest at least 15 minutes before rolling or wrap in plastic wrap and store in the refrigerator for up to 24 hours.

   By hand: Chop the spinach as finely as possible with a knife. Combine it in a mixing bowl with the egg and semolina and stir until well blended. Pile ⅔ cup of the flour on the work table and make a well in the center. Turn the spinach mixture out into the well and work in the flour with a kneading action. When the mixture begins to feel dry, gather it into a ball and set it aside. Scrape the table with a pastry scraper and sift the flour you scrape up back onto the table, discarding any small bits of dough. Knead the dough, adding more flour if necessary, until it is smooth and slightly sticky. Let the dough rest a few minutes before rolling.

3. Roll out and cut the dough as directed in individual recipes.

Variation: Egg Noodle Dough
Ordinary yellow noodles are made in the same way as Spinach Noodle Dough, but without the spinach. Start with 2 eggs and ⅔ cup semolina and add ⅔ to 1 cup all-purpose flour.

Technique Note In either recipe, using entirely all-purpose flour will make more tender noodles that cook even more quickly.

Tagliarini with Shrimp in Lemon Cream Sauce

Briefly infusing warm cream with lemon peel gives a subtle lemon scent to this creamy sauce for thin pasta. Finely dicing the shrimp allows their flavor to go farther, and the small pink flecks are more in keeping with the delicacy of the dish than whole shrimp would be. You can substitute other mild herbs, such as lemon thyme, dill, or chervil, for the chives.

Serves 6

> 1 large or 2 small lemons
> 1 cup whipping cream
> ½ pound shrimp (any size), peeled and deveined
> 1 recipe Egg Noodle Dough (left),
>   cut into thin, narrow noodles (tagliarini)
>   OR ½ pound thin dried pasta (cappelli or
>   vermicelli)
> 1 tablespoon unsalted butter
> Kosher salt and freshly ground black pepper to
>   taste
> 2 teaspoons chopped chives

1. Remove the lemon zest with a peeler, taking only the yellow part, and cut it into fine julienne shreds. Or use a zester, which removes the zest in thin strips. Combine the cream and 1 tablespoon of the zest in a small saucepan. Bring almost to a boil, remove from the heat, and let stand 15 to 30 minutes.

2. Juice the lemon(s) and toss the shrimp in 1 table-spoon of the juice. Let stand 5 minutes and drain. Split the shrimp lengthwise and cut the halves crosswise into ¼-inch pieces. (Medium shrimp will produce about 10 pieces each, large shrimp 12 to 14.)

3. Bring a large pot of lightly salted water to a boil. If us-ing dried pasta, start cooking the pasta before cooking the sauce; fresh pasta will cook in a minute or so when the sauce is nearly done.

4. Melt the butter in a large skillet over medium-low heat. Add the diced shrimp, salt, and pepper and cook just until the shrimp begins to color. Remove the shrimp with a slotted spoon and set aside. Add the cream and chives and bring to a boil. If using fresh pasta, start boiling it at this point. Cook the sauce until reduced by about a third. Drain the pasta and add it to the sauce. (Do not overdrain — see Technique Note, page 67.) Add the shrimp and toss the pasta to coat it with the sauce. Serve immediately on warmed plates.

Spaghettini with Shrimp and Broccoli

In her book *Modern Italian Cooking*, restaurateur Biba Caggiano of Sacramento, California gives a recipe for "a peasant dish that now enjoys a resurgent popularity in Italy"—pasta with broccoli, hot peppers, and anchovies. Adding shrimp not only takes this dish out of the peasant-food category, it makes it into a more substantial dish, which can also serve as a main course for 3 or 4.

Serves 6

> *½ pound medium shrimp, peeled, split lengthwise, and deveined*
> *Kosher salt and freshly ground black pepper*
> *1 pound broccoli*
> *½ pound spaghettini, vermicelli, or other thin dried pasta*
> *4 tablespoons everyday olive oil (see Note)*
> *1 clove garlic, lightly smashed*
> *2 anchovy fillets, rinsed and chopped*
> *   OR 1 teaspoon anchovy paste*
> *½ teaspoon red pepper flakes*
> *¼ teaspoon kosher salt*
> *2 tablespoons extra-virgin olive oil*

1. Sprinkle the shrimp with a little salt and pepper and set aside. Trim the tough ends from the broccoli and thinly slice the stalks crosswise, starting from the stem end. As you cut, the florets will fall away. Trim the long stems of the florets and cut the larger ones into bite-sized pieces. Blanch or steam the florets and stalk pieces separately until just tender but still crunchy. Rinse with cold water to stop the cooking.

2. Boil the pasta in ample salted water. Meanwhile, combine the oil, garlic, anchovy, red pepper, and salt in a large skillet and cook over medium-low heat until fragrant. Discard the garlic, add the shrimp and broccoli, and cook, stirring, until the shrimp are opaque. If the sauce is done before the pasta is ready, remove it from the heat.

3. Drain the pasta and add it to the pan. (Do not overdrain—see Technique Note, page 67.) Sprinkle in the extra-virgin oil, toss to coat the pasta with the sauce, and serve immediately on warmed plates.

Note Using two different olive oils here is not an affectation. When heated for more than a few seconds, a fine extra-virgin oil will lose much of its special fragrance, so I use a cheaper, milder oil for the cooking stage. When added at the end, the more flavorful oil acts as a flavoring and perfuming agent rather than as a cooking medium.

Technique Note If you have a pasta pot with a separate steamer basket, you can steam the broccoli over the same water you will use to cook the pasta. Don't blanch broccoli in the same water, however, or it will give a boiled-broccoli smell and taste to the pasta.

Risotto di Frutti di Mare
(Mixed Shellfish Risotto)

Risotto, rice cooked by a uniquely Italian technique, provides a smooth, richly textured background for all sorts of savory flavors. *Frutti di mare*, literally "fruits of the sea," is shorthand for an assortment of shellfish that is a marvel of kitchen synergy. Just as a blend of grapes gives complexity to some wines, so a combination of shrimp, squid, and clams or mussels produces a flavor that exceeds the sum of its parts.

Here are two shellfish risotti from opposite ends of Italy. The first is based on a dish I ate in Venice, against which I have measured all seafood risotto since. I also like the second version, from Taranto, for its zesty combination of tomatoes and the red pepper flakes so popular throughout southern Italy.

From the time you begin cooking the squid, the risotto needs more or less constant attention for 25 to 30 minutes, so keep the rest of the menu simple.

Risotto di Frutti di Mare alla Veneziana

Serves 6

> *½ pound squid (including tentacles), cleaned*
> *4 cups (approximately) unsalted chicken stock*
> *   or Quick Shrimp Stock (see page 113)*
> *3 tablespoons olive oil*
> *2 tablespoons finely chopped shallots or onion*
> *1⅓ cups Arborio rice (see Note)*
> *¼ cup dry white wine*
> *Scant teaspoon kosher salt*
> *Black pepper to taste*
> *12 small clams or mussels in the shell, scrubbed*
> *¼ pound small or medium shrimp, peeled*
> *   and deveined*
> *¼ pound small scallops*
> *1 cup fresh or frozen peas*

1. Set aside the squid tentacles; remove the spotted skin from the sacs and mince the meat as finely as possible. Have the stock at a simmer and a large ladle at hand.

2. Heat the oil in a medium-sized heavy saucepan and sauté the shallots and minced squid for 2 minutes. Stir in the rice and cook another minute or two, coating it thoroughly with the oil. Add the wine and enough stock just to cover. Stir in the salt and pepper and cook *uncovered*, stirring frequently, until the liquid is nearly absorbed.

3. Add stock a ladleful at a time, cooking until each addition is almost absorbed before adding the next. Stir occasionally. Once the rice has begun to swell and lose its translucency, taste a grain. When only the very center still tastes raw, add a final ladleful of stock (there will probably be some left over) and set a timer for 10 minutes. Add the clams; if using mussels, add them when there are 7 minutes to go. Add the shrimp, scallops, and peas at 5 minutes and the squid tentacles at 1 minute. Check the seasoning and serve immediately.

Note Arborio rice is a special medium-grain rice from northern Italy, available in specialty stores and some supermarkets. If unavailable, substitute Calrose, a similar medium-grain rice from California. The results will be almost as good.

Risotto di Frutti de Mare alla Tarantina

Serves 6

Ingredients for Risotto di Frutti di Mare alla
*   Veneziana (page 64), except the peas*
2 cloves garlic, minced
Large pinch of red pepper flakes
1½ cups tomatoes, peeled, seeded, and chopped,
*   with their juice (if fresh tomatoes are not at*
*   their peak, use good canned tomatoes)*
1 teaspoon chopped fresh marjoram
*   OR ¼ teaspoon dried marjoram*

Follow the previous recipe, adding the garlic and red pepper flakes with the shallots and squid in step 2. Add the tomatoes and marjoram and cook 5 minutes. Stir in the rice, add the wine and stock to cover, and continue as above.

Shrimp Cakes

This is an adaptation of the crab cakes so popular throughout the Southeast and mid-Atlantic states. Although the cakes are rather small, they are rich, so two per person is an ample serving. If you must have a sauce, tartar sauce is traditional.

Serves 4

1 pound shrimp (any size), cooked and peeled
2 cups soft bread crumbs
4 to 5 tablespoons mayonnaise
½ cup thinly sliced green onions
2 tablespoons chopped parsley
1 teaspoon Chesapeake-style seafood seasoning
*   (see page 38)*
1 heaping tablespoon dried shrimp (optional)
All-purpose flour for dipping (about ½ cup)
1 egg, lightly beaten
2 tablespoons oil or clarified butter

1. Cut the shrimp into long shreds and combine them in a bowl with 1 cup of the bread crumbs and 4 tablespoons of the mayonnaise. Add the green onions, parsley, and seasoning mix. If using the dried shrimp, pound them in a mortar to fine threads and add them to the shrimp mixture. Stir to combine the ingredients, adding a little more mayonnaise if necessary to bind everything.

2. Form the shrimp mixture into 8 patties about ¾ inch thick. Dredge the patties in flour, dip in egg, and roll in the remaining bread crumbs. The cakes may be prepared to this point up to an hour ahead and refrigerated. Remove from the refrigerator 15 minutes before cooking.

3. Heat the oil in a large skillet and cook the cakes over medium-low heat until golden brown and heated through, about 5 minutes per side. Serve with lemon wedges.

Pasta and Shrimp with Mint Pesto

Pesto, the fragrant Genovese basil and garlic sauce, is not a traditional partner to seafood in Italian cooking, but I think they make a great color and flavor combination. This recipe uses a lesser known version of pesto, made with fresh mint rather than basil. Most pesto also contains grated cheese, but as cheese and seafood are rarely combined in Italian pasta dishes, this version is cheeseless. An old-fashioned mortar and pestle makes the best pesto, and when you count cleaning-up time, a small batch mixed by hand takes no more time than it takes to use a food processor or blender.

Serves 6

> *1 recipe Egg Noodle Dough (see page 60),*
>   *cut into fettuccine or tagliarini*
>   *OR ½ pound dried linguine or perciatelli*
> *1 tablespoon unsalted butter or olive oil*
> *½ pound small or medium shrimp, peeled,*
>   *deveined, and salt-leached (see page 16)*
> *Freshly ground black pepper*

> **MINT PESTO**
> *1 large clove garlic, peeled*
> *1 cup (loosely packed) fresh mint leaves, torn*
>   *into small pieces*
> *⅛ teaspoon kosher salt*
> *8 whole blanched almonds OR 1 heaping*
>   *tablespoon blanched slivered almonds*
> *¼ cup olive oil*

1. To make the mint pesto, pound the garlic, mint, salt, and nuts together in a mortar to a paste. Stir in the oil a little at a time. To make in a blender or food processor, simply combine all the ingredients and process to a smooth paste, stopping frequently to scrape the sides of the jar. Keep covered until ready to use. (Makes ⅓ cup.)

2. Bring a large pot of lightly salted water to a boil. If using dried pasta, start cooking the pasta before cooking the shrimp; fresh pasta will cook in a minute or so when the shrimp are nearly done.

3. Heat the butter or oil over low heat in a large skillet. Add the shrimp and a sprinkling of pepper and cook gently until the shrimp turn opaque. If the shrimp get done before the pasta, remove the pan from the heat.

4. Drain the pasta quickly and add it to the skillet. Add the pesto and stir to coat the pasta and shrimp with the sauce. Serve immediately on warm plates.

Technique Note Do not drain the pasta too thoroughly; in this, as in many pasta dishes, a tablespoon or two of water left clinging to the noodles becomes a part of the sauce. It's a secret ingredient known to many experienced pasta cooks.

Entrées

Shrimp with Asparagus
   and Pancetta
Shrimp and Leek Tart
Stir-Fried Shrimp with
   Sugar Snap Peas
Shrimp Chow Mein with
   Bok Choy
Tempura
Shrimp Benedict
Salt and Pepper Prawns
Thai Green Curried Shrimp
Bombay Shrimp Curry
Boudins de Fruits de Mer
Shrimp and Asparagus Frittata
Louisiana Shrimp Boil
Baked Stuffed Shrimp
Rock Shrimp Soufflé
Shrimp Salad Sandwich
Poached Halibut with
   Shrimp Sauce
Beer Batter Fried Shrimp
Mariko's Teppan Yaki
Shrimp Scampi-Style
Shrimp Broiled in Butter
Shrimp and Corn Pot Pies
Budín de Mariscos
Garidópita
Shrimp Creole

Shrimp Broiled in Butter

Shrimp with Asparagus and Pancetta

This is something of a show-off dish. If yours is the kind of kitchen where everyone gathers before dinner, your guests will be impressed by how you pull all the elements together at the last minute. Actually, it's not very difficult, once you understand the timing, and several of the components can be prepared ahead. The finished dish is absolutely delicious. Deeply flavorful, woodsy mushrooms play off the bright taste and color of the shrimp, slightly crunchy asparagus, and intensely flavored nuggets of *pancetta*. A hint of aged vinegar rounds and lightens the overall effect.

Serves 4

> *4 large dried black mushrooms (see Note)*
> *2 cups unsalted chicken stock*
> *2 teaspoons soy sauce*
> *Pinch of sugar*
> *1 teaspoon balsamic vinegar or Chinese black*
> *   (Chekiang or Chinkiang) vinegar*
> *½ teaspoon cornstarch dissolved in 2 teaspoons*
> *   cold water*
> *1 ounce thinly sliced pancetta (Italian-style*
> *   unsmoked bacon), cut into fine shreds*
> *2 tablespoons oil*
> *1 pound medium or large shrimp, peeled*
> *   and deveined*
> *1 tablespoon minced shallots*
> *24 pencil-thin asparagus spears, 5 to 6 inches long*

1. Soak the mushrooms in lukewarm water until soft, at least 30 minutes. Drain, reserving the liquid. Remove and discard the stems and slice the caps as thinly as possible. In a small saucepan, combine the mushrooms, ½ cup of the stock, the soy sauce, the sugar, and ½ teaspoon of the vinegar. Bring to a boil, simmer 10 minutes, remove from the heat, and let steep 15 minutes to several hours.

2. Bring the remaining stock to a boil in another saucepan, reduce to a lively simmer, and cook down to about ½ cup. Set aside. Dissolve the cornstarch in the water and set aside.

3. Have a pot of simmering salted water ready to cook the asparagus. Cook the pancetta slowly in a large skillet until crisp. Remove and drain on paper towels; discard the drippings. Add the oil to the skillet and cook the shrimp over medium-high heat until pink. Remove and keep warm. Add the shallots to the skillet and cook until translucent. Meanwhile, start cooking the asparagus. Add the mushrooms and their steeping liquid and the reduced stock to the skillet, turn the heat to high, and boil down the sauce slightly. Stir the cornstarch mixture and add it to the sauce; cook until the sauce is glossy and slightly thickened. Add the remaining ½ teaspoon of vinegar and taste the sauce for seasoning.

4. When the asparagus are tender, after about 4 minutes of cooking, arrange them on individual plates or a serving platter. Return the shrimp to the skillet to coat them with sauce, then arrange them on the plates opposite the asparagus. Place the mushrooms between the shrimp and asparagus in the center of the plates and spoon the sauce over all. Scatter the pancetta on top.

Note The dried, crinkly-capped black mushrooms known as *shiitake* in Japanese are available wherever Asian foods are sold. The more lacy cracks in the caps, the better the quality. I much prefer the imported dried variety to the fresh shiitake cultivated here.

Shrimp and Leek Tart

This savory pastry was inspired by *pissaladière*, the onion and olive tart of southern France. With a salad, a few olives, a glass of wine, and fresh fruit for dessert, it makes a perfect lunch or light supper.

Serves 6

>*2 pounds leeks*
>*2 tablespoons olive oil*
>*1 cup water*
>*Kosher salt and pepper to taste*
>*2 tablespoons flour*
>*¾ pound small or medium shrimp, peeled*
>* and deveined*
>
>**TART SHELL**
>*1 cup plus 2 tablespoons all-purpose flour*
>*¼ pound cold unsalted butter, cut into*
>* 1-inch pieces*
>*⅛ teaspoon kosher salt*
>*⅓ cup cold water*

1. Prepare the tart dough as follows: Combine the flour, butter, and salt in a food processor or electric mixer and blend until the mixture resembles coarse meal. With the motor running, add the water in a thin stream just until the dough begins to come together. (You may not need all the water.) Gather the dough by hand into a ball, wrap tightly, and refrigerate at least 15 minutes.

2. Wash the leeks, but don't worry about getting every bit of dirt off at this point. Trim off the root ends and loose green top leaves. Starting at the root end, cut the stalks crosswise into slices about ⅛ inch thick. When the outer leaves are more green than yellow, remove them and continue slicing the paler centers. You should have about 4 cups of slices.

3. Transfer the slices to a large bowl of water and separate them into rings. Swirl the water to wash away any dirt and let stand a few minutes for the dirt to settle to the bottom. Lift the leeks out of the water and into a heavy saucepan. (Do not drain through a colander; that would defeat the purpose of soaking them.) Add the oil and 1 cup water. Bring to a boil, reduce to a simmer, and cook uncovered until the liquid is nearly gone and the leeks are quite soft, about 45 minutes. Season to taste with salt and pepper.

4. While the leeks are cooking, roll out the dough and use it to line a 10-inch tart pan; use a double thickness of dough for the sides and trim away any excess. Return the shell to the refrigerator for 15 minutes. Then line the inside of the shell with heavy aluminum foil and fill it with dried beans or pie weights. Bake in the upper part of a 400° oven for 15 minutes, remove the foil and beans, and continue baking until light golden brown, another 5 to 10 minutes.

5. Sprinkle the flour inside the tart shell and arrange the shrimp over it. Spread the leek mixture over all, pressing it down into the spaces between the shrimp and around the edges. Bake 15 minutes, or until the shrimp are fully cooked. Serve warm.

Technique Note Despite the many books that insist you cannot make a good, reliable flaky dough with all butter and American flour, this one, developed by San Francisco pastry chef Jim Dodge, works just fine. The key is to avoid overworking the dough; if you let the machine run until the dough completely pulls together, the shell will shrink and crack as it bakes and the crust will be tough. Minor cracks can be patched with a little reserved dough after removing the foil, but large cracks will result in the filling running out in the oven.

Stir-Fried Shrimp with Sugar Snap Peas

Tender, pink shrimp with crunchy, bright green snow peas are a Chinese restaurant favorite. This version substitutes another delicious edible-pod pea, the more compact, rounded "sugar snap" variety. To preserve the brilliant pink color of the shrimp, this recipe does not use soy sauce. Along with rice, it makes a one-dish meal; or you can combine it with other Chinese dishes for a multicourse meal for four or more. (Chicken simmered in soy sauce would be an ideal partner.)

Serves 2

> ¾ pound small or medium shrimp, peeled,
>   deveined, and salt-leached (see page 16)
> ¾ teaspoon cornstarch
> ½ cup unsalted chicken stock
> 2 tablespoons peanut oil
> 1 heaping teaspoon minced ginger
> Pinch of kosher salt
> Pinch of white pepper
> ½ pound (about 3 cups) sugar snap peas, stems
>   and strings removed
> ½ red bell pepper, seeded and cut into
>   1-inch squares

> **MARINADE**
> ¼ cup dry sherry or Chinese rice wine
> 1 tablespoon cornstarch
> 1 teaspoon minced ginger

1. Combine the shrimp and the marinade ingredients, stir to combine, and let stand 15 minutes to 1 hour. (The time doesn't make any difference in flavor; it's more a matter of convenience.)

2. Drain the shrimp and discard the marinade. Dissolve the cornstarch in the stock and set aside.

3. Place a wok or large skillet over high heat and add 1 tablespoon oil and the ginger, salt, and pepper. When the ginger sizzles, add the drained shrimp and stir-fry just until they begin to stiffen and turn opaque. Transfer with a large spoon to a plate and set aside.

4. Add the remaining oil to the pan, add the peas and red pepper, and stir-fry until heated through. Stir the stock mixture to dissolve the cornstarch and add it to the pan. Return the shrimp to the pan and cook, stirring, until the sauce is thick and glossy, about 1 minute. Serve immediately.

Shrimp Chow Mein with Bok Choy

If you associate chow mein with canned fried noodles, you'll be pleasantly surprised when you try the real thing. A tangled mat of noodles, crisp and browned on the outside, is the perfect vehicle for the well-sauced stir-fried dish that tops it. In this version, sweet, pink shrimp contrast with the mildly bitter, deep green and white Chinese cabbage known as bok choy.

Serves 2

½ pound thin Chinese-style noodles
OR 6 ounces dried egg tagliarini
4 tablespoons oil
1 cup unsalted chicken stock
2 tablespoons soy sauce
1½ teaspoons cornstarch
1 tablespoon minced ginger
4 green onions, in ¾-inch diagonal slices
½ pound medium shrimp, peeled, split lengthwise, deveined, and salt-leached (see page 16)
2 cups sliced bok choy stems and leaves
½ cup sliced bamboo shoots

1. Cook the noodles according to package directions. Drain, rinse with cold water to stop the cooking, and drain thoroughly. Toss with 1 tablespoon of oil to keep them from sticking together.

2. Heat 1 tablespoon of oil in a 10-inch skillet (heavy nonstick or well-seasoned cast iron). Add half the noodles to the pan, forming them into a thick "pancake." Cook until well browned on the underside, about 4 minutes, then loosen and turn with a large spatula. Brown well on the other side, then transfer to a dinner plate and keep warm in a 200° oven. Repeat with the remaining noodles.

3. Combine the stock, soy sauce, and cornstarch and stir to dissolve. Heat a wok over medium-high heat and add 1 tablespoon of oil. Add the ginger and green onions and cook until fragrant. Add the shrimp and stir-fry 1 minute, or until they begin to stiffen and curl. Add the bok choy and bamboo shoots and stir-fry until heated through. Add the stock mixture, bring to a boil, and cook until the sauce is thick and glossy.

4. Arrange the shrimp mixture on top of the noodle pancakes and spoon the sauce over all. Unless you are especially skilled with chopsticks, serve this dish with forks.

Technique Note Resist the temptation to dirty one less pan by using the same pan for frying the noodles and stir-frying the shrimp mixture. It's very difficult to make a neat, flat noodle pancake in a wok, nor is a typical skillet deep enough to properly stir-fry a mound of leafy vegetables.

Tempura

Japanese tempura is perhaps the most refined form of deep-frying. To achieve the delicate, lacy coating of crisp batter that is the hallmark of good tempura, speed is of the essence in both cooking and serving. The ideal setup is a counter near the stove, where you can serve the fried tidbits immediately and directly to your guests. Be warned, however—as the cook, you will be too busy to eat until all the food is cooked. Rather than make everyone wait until everything is done, resign yourself to eating last. Maybe you can recruit another cook to take over partway through so you can sit down and enjoy some fresh from the pan.

Serves 4

> *½ pound medium shrimp, butterflied*
> *Sliced vegetables—an assortment of the following:*
> > *small eggplant, thickly sliced crosswise*
> > *large mushrooms, thickly sliced vertically*
> > *red, yellow, or green bell peppers, sliced*
> > > *crosswise and seeded*
> > *zucchini or other summer squash, sliced*
> > > *diagonally*
> > *sweet potatoes (red or yellow fleshed), thinly*
> > > *sliced crosswise*
> > *thick green onions, in 1-inch sections*
> > *tender green beans, in 2-inch sections*
> *Soy-Ginger Dipping Sauce (see page 112)*
> > *OR soy sauce and seasoned rice vinegar*
> *Oil for deep-frying*
> *1 large egg yolk*
> *1¼ cups cold water*
> *1 cup sifted all-purpose flour*

1. Lay out the shrimp and vegetables on a tray or platter. Set them close to the stove, leaving space for the batter bowl. Set out individual bowls of dipping sauce, or dilute seasoned rice vinegar with an equal amount of water and set it out in small pitchers to be mixed with soy sauce for dipping.

2. Heat the oil in a deep frying pan (a wok is ideal) to 350°, then turn the heat down to low. Beat the egg yolk and water together in a bowl until foamy; dump in the flour and stir with chopsticks just until blended but still lumpy.

3. Two or three pieces at a time, drop the shrimp and vegetables into the batter. With chopsticks or tongs, lift each piece out of the batter, letting the excess drain back into the bowl, and slip it into the hot oil. After adding the first pieces to the oil, turn the heat to high. Continue battering pieces and adding them to the hot oil as many at a time as you can without crowding or cooling the oil. Turn the pieces as necessary during cooking and retrieve each with a skimmer or chopsticks when golden brown (after about 3 minutes). Drain the pieces on paper towels and serve immediately on paper-lined plates, baskets, or trays. Standing the cooked shrimp and vegetables up on end keeps them crisp for a few moments longer, but they should still be eaten as soon as possible.

Technique Note The ideal slicing thickness for each vegetable will result in the proper texture after cooking. Denser vegetables need to be sliced thinner, while those which cook to a soft texture quickly (especially eggplant) need to be cut thicker. The vegetables given here are listed in order of decreasing thickness, with zucchini as the median. Cut zucchini about ¼ inch thick, the rest somewhat thicker or somewhat thinner. If using other vegetables, consider the texture and cut accordingly.

Shrimp Benedict

In this twist on eggs Benedict, a ring of cooked shrimp replaces the traditional slice of Canadian bacon. A slimmed-down version of hollandaise sauce, made with a whole egg and pureed ricotta in place of some of the egg yolks, cuts down on both calories and cholesterol. You can poach the eggs according to your favorite method or use mine. Add some fresh fruit and a basket of assorted whole-grain muffins to complete the menu.

Serves 6

1 cup unsalted chicken stock
18 medium shrimp
1 quart water (approximately)
Pinch of kosher salt
1 tablespoon vinegar
6 large eggs, at room temperature
6 toasted English muffin halves
2 cups plain or marinated artichoke hearts,
    well drained

BLENDER MOCK HOLLANDAISE
1 large egg
1 large egg yolk
2 tablespoons part-skim ricotta
1 tablespoon lemon juice
Pinch of kosher salt
White or cayenne pepper to taste
1½ ounces (3 tablespoons) unsalted butter or
    Shrimp Butter (see page 112)

1. Bring the chicken stock to a simmer in a small saucepan. Add the shrimp and simmer (do not boil) until the meat is opaque, about 5 minutes. Remove the shrimp with a slotted spoon. As soon as they are cool enough to handle, peel the shrimp, returning the shells to the stock. Devein the shrimp if necessary and keep them warm.

2. Prepare the sauce as follows: Combine the egg, egg yolk, ricotta, lemon juice, salt, and pepper in a blender and blend thoroughly. Stop to scrape the sides of the jar occasionally to incorporate every bit of ricotta smoothly into the sauce. Meanwhile, melt the butter and keep it warm, just short of the bubbling stage. Strain the shrimp-flavored stock into a heat-proof measuring cup. With the blender running at high speed, add the butter to the egg mixture in a thin stream. Add ¼ cup of the stock in a thin stream. Reserve the remaining stock for another use. Taste the sauce for seasoning and correct if necessary. Transfer the sauce to a heatproof measuring pitcher or bowl and place it in a warm water bath while cooking the eggs.

3. Bring the water just to a boil in a deep skillet and add the salt and vinegar. Reduce to a simmer. Add the eggs *in the shell* to the simmering water; after 15 seconds remove them with a slotted spoon. Crack one egg at a time into a small bowl and gently slide it into the water. Cook the eggs, never letting the water boil, until the whites are set and the yolks are glazed over but still liquid, about 3 minutes. Meanwhile, place the English muffins on individual warm plates and arrange the shrimp on top, tails pointing inward.

4. Retrieve the poached eggs with a slotted spoon. (Try to do this in the order they were added to the pan, so they all get roughly the same amount of cooking time; an easy way is to start both cooking and retrieving at the same position in the pan, say nearest the handle, and work in a circle.) Trim off any loose bits of white and nestle an egg in the center of each ring of shrimp. Nap each portion with 2 to 3 tablespoons of the sauce and serve, garnished with artichoke hearts.

→

Variation Other vegetables may be substituted for the artichoke hearts. Try asparagus tips, sautéed julienne zucchini or yellow squash, cherry tomatoes or tomato wedges, snow peas, or sugar snap peas.

Technique Note This recipe will result in leftover stock as well as sauce, but it's really not practical to make either in any smaller quantity. Save the shrimp-flavored stock for other purposes; the sauce doesn't keep well and will need to be discarded.

Salt and Pepper Prawns

This is one of the simplest and most delicious shrimp dishes in the Chinese repertoire. The shells are an important part of the dish; besides tempering the heat so the meat will cook more evenly, they protect the meat from too strong a dose of salt and pepper, much of which ends up clinging to the shells. To eat shell-on shrimp in true Chinese style, take a whole shrimp into your mouth with chopsticks, work the meat out of the shell by whatever combination of teeth and tongue will do the job, and remove the shell with your chopsticks. If you lack the necessary oral dexterity, use your fingers to hold the shrimp by the tail and pick out the meat with chopsticks; or give up on utensils altogether and eat with your fingers. Another option, especially with the smallest shrimp, is to eat shell and all.

Serves 4

> *2 tablespoons oil*
> *1 pound small to medium shrimp, deveined*
>   *through the shell*
> *1 teaspoon kosher salt*
> *1 teaspoon freshly ground black pepper*

Heat a wok or large skillet over high heat. Add the oil in a thin stream around the edge of the pan, letting it run into the center. Add the shrimp and stir-fry until the shells turn pink, about 2 minutes. Add the salt and pepper and continue cooking until all the shrimp meat is opaque. Keep the mixture moving constantly so the shrimp cook evenly and the seasonings are well distributed. Serve with rice and a colorful vegetable dish.

Thai Green Curried Shrimp

Thai curries are based on curry paste, a pounded or blended mixture of wet and dry ingredients. They vary from merely hot to incendiary, depending on how much of the chile seeds and ribs you include in the paste. This version is relatively mild.

Serves 4

> 3 slices fresh or dried galingale (see page 48)
> 6 small green chiles, stems removed
> 1 stalk lemongrass (bottom half only),
>   thinly sliced and minced
> 1 teaspoon grated lime peel
> 2 cloves garlic, peeled
> 3 tablespoons minced shallot
>   OR 3 green onions, minced
> 6 sprigs fresh coriander (cilantro)
> 1 teaspoon ground coriander seed
> ½ teaspoon kosher salt
> 3 tablespoons oil
> 2 tablespoons lime juice
> 1 can (14 ounces) unsweetened coconut milk,
>   skimmed (see Note)
> 1 cup finely diced sweet potato, coarsely diced
>   eggplant, or a combination
> ¾ to 1 pound medium or large shrimp, peeled and
>   deveined
> 2 tablespoons fish sauce (see page 111)
> ½ teaspoon sugar
> Fresh coriander, mint, or basil leaves, for garnish

1. If using dried galingale, soak it in hot water until it can be cut easily with a knife. Drain and mince as finely as possible. (Or skip the soaking and grind the pieces in a spice grinder; see Technique Note.) Split the chiles and remove the ribs and seeds.

2. In a blender, combine the galingale, chiles, lemongrass, lime peel, garlic, shallot, coriander, coriander seed, salt, oil, and lime juice. Blend to a paste.

3. Transfer the contents of the blender to a wok or skillet and place it over medium heat. Cook until the mixture is bubbly and quite fragrant and the oil begins to separate from the paste. Add the coconut milk and diced vegetables and simmer (do not boil) until the vegetables are just tender, about 5 minutes. Add the shrimp, fish sauce, and sugar and cook until the shrimp are opaque. Transfer to a serving bowl, garnish with the fresh herbs, and serve with rice.

Note Canned coconut milk varies from one brand to another in fat content. Sometimes up to half the can is the thick "cream" which rises to the top. Since that cream is almost entirely saturated fat, skim off and discard as much of it as your conscience dictates and add water to what remains to make 1½ cups. The resulting "thin" coconut milk will have plenty of coconut flavor.

Technique Note The traditional way to make curry pastes is to pound the ingredients together in a mortar. No other tool does as thorough a job of mashing and grinding all the ingredients together, and it works surprisingly quickly. If you don't have one or the patience to use it, a blender or mini-chopper does the job more effectively than a food processor. An electric spice grinder is also handy for preliminary grinding of coriander seeds, lemongrass, dried galingale, and other hard ingredients.

Bombay Shrimp Curry

In the United States, coconut milk is associated mainly with Thai and other Southeast Asian cuisines. But coconut milk and oil are just as common in the cooking of southern India. This simple curry is typical of the coastal regions from Bombay southward along the Malabar Coast. It can be made gentle or hot, depending on the amount of cayenne pepper you use. It is quite soupy and should be served with plenty of rice.

Serves 4

> 1 pound medium shrimp, peeled and deveined
> 1 teaspoon kosher salt
> 2 tablespoons oil
> 1½ cups diced onion
> 2 cloves garlic, minced
> 1 teaspoon minced or grated ginger
> ¾ teaspoon ground turmeric
> ⅛ to ¼ teaspoon cayenne pepper
> 1 can (14 ounces) unsweetened coconut milk
> 1 teaspoon tamarind concentrate dissolved in
>   2 tablespoons warm water (see Note)
> 2 or 3 small fresh chiles, sliced, loose seeds removed
> 2 tablespoons fresh coriander leaves (cilantro)

1. Toss the shrimp with ½ teaspoon salt and set aside.

2. Heat the oil in a wok or deep skillet over medium-low heat. Add the onion, garlic, ginger, remaining salt, turmeric, and cayenne pepper and cook until the onion begins to brown.

3. Discard some of the cream from the coconut milk, if desired (see Note, page 83), and add enough water to make 2 cups. Add to the pan along with the tamarind liquid, heat to just short of boiling, and reduce to a simmer. Add the shrimp and sliced chiles and cook until the shrimp are opaque, about 7 minutes. Stir in the coriander leaves and serve with rice.

Note Tamarind is a sourish pulp extracted from the seed pods of the tropical tamarind tree and widely used as a tart ingredient in South Asian and Latin American cooking. This recipe calls for the paste-like tamarind concentrate sold in jars in Indian groceries. Southeast Asian markets sell another form, semisolid blocks complete with seeds and fibers. If using the latter, dissolve 2 teaspoons in 2 tablespoons of water and strain before adding to the curry. If no tamarind is available, use lemon or lime juice to taste.

Boudins de Fruits de Mer
(Seafood Sausages)

Seafood sausages became all the rage in French *nouvelle cuisine* a few years back, and they remain popular as an elegant low-calorie dish. They are surprisingly easy to make. When a seafood quenelle mixture is cooked in an enclosed space (such as a sausage casing), it emerges not as a lighter-than-air dumpling, but firm like a good sausage.

Leftover sausages freeze well, so consider making a double batch and freezing the leftovers. Reheat them in a steamer, or try them sliced and browned and added to a marinara sauce for pasta.

Makes about 16 sausages

> *¾ cup medium-grain rice, such as Calrose*
> *   or Italian Arborio*
> *2 cups water or unsalted fish stock*
> *1 pound small shrimp, peeled and deveined*
> *1 pound fillet of halibut, flounder, sole,*
> *   or other flatfish*
> *½ pound scallops*
> *1 teaspoon minced fresh ginger*
> *2 green onions, sliced*
> *2 teaspoons kosher salt*
> *¼ teaspoon white pepper*
> *Large pinch of cayenne pepper*
> *2 large egg whites*

1. Cook the rice, uncovered, in the water or stock until it is quite tender and no liquid remains. Chill.

2. In a food processor, combine the rice, half the shrimp, and all the remaining ingredients except the egg whites; blend to a light, fluffy paste. Stop periodically to scrape down the sides of the bowl. With the motor running, add the egg whites through the feed tube. Continue processing until the egg whites are entirely incorporated. Chop the remaining shrimp finely by hand and stir it in. Poach a teaspoonful of the mixture in lightly salted water until it floats; taste for seasoning and adjust if necessary. Chill until ready to roll.

3. Brush a 6 × 7-inch rectangle of aluminum foil lightly with oil. Spoon about 3 tablespoons of the fish mixture down the center of the foil. Roll the mixture back and forth in the foil, as if rolling a cigarette, until you have a cylinder 1 inch in diameter. Flatten the ends of the foil and roll them tightly inward to form a firm cylindrical "sausage." Repeat with the rest of the fish mixture. Refrigerate rolls until ready to cook.

4. Steam the sausages in a perforated steamer basket for 10 minutes. Allow them to cool slightly, then unwrap them and trim off any loose edges. Serve 2 whole sausages as a seafood first course, or slice the sausages into bite-sized pieces to serve with toothpicks as an hors d'oeuvre. Serve with a flavored mayonnaise or, in summer, with a fresh tomato sauce.

Note The mixture of fish and shellfish can be varied within a certain range. Mild white fish gives an even consistency and acts as a background for stronger shellfish flavors. Scallops add a lot of body as well as sweet flavor. A little bit of squid makes an inexpensive stretcher, but use no more than about 20 percent squid or that's all you will taste. You can use lobster meat in place of shrimp.

Shrimp and Asparagus Frittata

A frittata is an Italian-style open-faced omelette which can serve as a vehicle for all sorts of savory ingredients. The potatoes in this version are inspired by its Spanish cousin, the *tortilla española.* Unlike a French omelette, which must be served immediately after cooking, a frittata is even better lukewarm or at room temperature. Try it as a light supper entrée, an appetizer before grilled meats or fish, or cut up into small wedges as a cocktail nibble.

Serves 4

>3 tablespoons olive oil
>2 small red-skinned potatoes, sliced ⅛ inch thick
>Pinch of kosher salt
>¼ pound fresh asparagus, trimmed
>6 large eggs, at room temperature
>¼ pound tiny cooked and peeled shrimp
>1 ounce thinly sliced prosciutto
>   or other full-flavored ham, cut into slivers
>Freshly ground black pepper to taste

1. Heat 2 tablespoons of the oil in a 10-inch skillet (nonstick or well-seasoned cast iron) over medium-low heat. Add the potato slices and cook until tender and lightly browned, about 10 minutes. Sprinkle with salt and remove the pan from the heat. While the potatoes are cooking, steam or boil the asparagus until just tender and cut into 1-inch lengths.

2. Beat the eggs lightly in a large bowl. Add the asparagus, shrimp, prosciutto, and pepper. Remove the potatoes from the skillet with a slotted spoon and add them to the eggs. Stir to coat everything evenly with egg. Add the remaining tablespoon of oil to the skillet and return it to medium heat. Pour in the egg mixture, spreading the vegetables and shrimp evenly in the pan. Cook until the egg is set around the edges but still runny in the center, about 5 minutes, then run the pan under the broiler for a minute or two to brown the top and finish cooking the egg. If the center is still moist after the top browns, return the pan to the stove top for another minute or so.

3. Slide the frittata out of the pan onto a platter. Serve hot, warm, or at room temperature, cut into wedges.

Louisiana Shrimp Boil

Next time you go on a summertime picnic, leave the hot dogs and steaks at home and bring along a big pot and the makings of a shrimp "boil." This is one-pot cooking at its most basic—whole shrimp, potatoes, onions, and corn on the cob simmered together in water liberally seasoned with whole spices and cayenne pepper. You can set up the boiling pot on a portable gas stove or on top of a built-in charcoal grill. Don't bother with a tablecloth; just spread the table with newspapers to receive the shrimp shells. (Of course, you can also cook this dish at home, on the stove.)

Serves 8 to 10

>2 gallons water
>½ cup vinegar
>¾ cup (about 3 ounces) pickling spices
>1 teaspoon cloves
>6 whole cardamom pods
>1 to 3 tablespoons cayenne pepper
>⅓ cup kosher salt
>2 lemons, quartered
>24 small new potatoes
>2 pounds onions, peeled and halved
>   (quartered if large)
>4 to 5 pounds shrimp, any size, head-on
>   or headless
>8 ears sweet corn, halved

1. In a large non-aluminum stockpot, combine the water, vinegar, whole spices (tied together in a square of cheesecloth for easy retrieval if you like), cayenne pepper, salt, and lemons and bring to a boil. Cook 5 minutes, then add the potatoes and onions. Boil 10 minutes, or until the potatoes feel almost done when probed with a skewer. Add the shrimp and corn, reduce the heat (if cooking over charcoal, move the pot away from the hottest part of the fire), and simmer until the shrimp are opaque and the corn is tender, about 8 minutes.

2. Drain through a colander and serve on platters or in large bowls. The cooking liquid may be strained and saved in the refrigerator for a week or so and used again. Serve with beer, iced tea, or lemonade.

Note In place of the spices, you can use a packaged "shrimp boil" such as Zatarain's. These mixes are available in a mesh bag of whole spices or as a clear liquid extract.

Baked Stuffed Shrimp

Although I grew up in the Northeast, I either never tried or had forgotten about this dish until I heard an ex-New Yorker in San Francisco waxing nostalgic over "bakedstuffedshrimp." A few years later, on a trip to New England, I found it on nearly every seafood restaurant menu. Unfortunately, some versions are more stuffing than shrimp. This one goes light on the stuffing, and instead of looking all alike, the shrimp come out with their tails pointing this way and that.

Serves 4

> *1 pound large or jumbo shrimp, butterflied*
>
> **STUFFING**
> *1 tablespoon oil or bacon drippings*
> *3 green onions, minced*
> *1 large clove garlic, minced*
> *1½ teaspoons chopped fresh herbs (marjoram,*
> *   thyme, Italian parsley, or a combination)*
> *   OR ¼ teaspoon crumbled dried herbs*
> *1 ounce sliced bacon, cooked and finely crumbled*
> *   (optional)*
> *¾ cup sifted fresh bread crumbs*
> *1 tablespoon grated Parmesan or Asiago cheese*
> *Kosher salt and freshly ground pepper to taste*

1. Prepare the stuffing as follows: Heat the oil in a small skillet and cook the onions, garlic, and herbs until the onions soften. Remove from the heat and combine with the remaining ingredients in a bowl.

2. Preheat the oven to 450°. Lay the shrimp in a lightly oiled baking dish, cut side down, with the tail shells pointing up. Spread a layer of stuffing over the flattened portion of each shrimp, mounding it slightly in the center. Bake until the shrimp are pink and the stuffing is well browned, 10 to 12 minutes. Serve with lemon wedges and, if a sauce is desired, tartar sauce or Rémoulade Sauce I (see page 110).

Rock Shrimp Soufflé

This dish was especially designed for the firm, lobster-like meat of Florida rock shrimp. It is equally delicious with other uncooked shrimp, but you may need to add salt, because the recipe takes into account the inherent saltiness of rock shrimp.

Serves 4

> 3 tablespoons unsalted butter or margarine
> ¼ cup finely grated Parmesan cheese
> 6 ounces uncooked rock shrimp meat
> 3 tablespoons flour
> 1 cup milk
> Pinch of cayenne pepper
> 4 large egg yolks, at room temperature
> 5 large egg whites, at room temperature

1. Using a teaspoon of the butter, lightly grease the inside of a 6-cup soufflé dish. Dust with cheese to coat evenly and shake out the excess.

2. Melt the remaining butter in a saucepan and cook the shrimp just until they turn pink. Remove them with a slotted spoon. Add the flour to the butter, stir, and cook over medium heat 3 to 5 minutes to make a pale roux. Add the milk and cayenne pepper and bring to a boil, stirring constantly. Reduce the heat and simmer until well thickened. Allow to cool slightly. Taste and correct seasoning.

3. Position an oven rack in the middle of the oven and preheat the oven to 400°. Return the shrimp to the sauce mixture and stir in the egg yolks. In a perfectly clean bowl, beat the egg whites to soft peaks. Stir a quarter of the egg whites into the sauce, then gently fold in the rest of the whites with a rubber spatula. Transfer to the soufflé dish and immediately place it in the oven. Reduce the heat to 375° and bake 25 to 30 minutes, or until a knife inserted in the center comes out clean. Serve immediately.

Shrimp Salad Sandwich

The rich-tasting but surprisingly low-calorie filling in this sandwich uses a favorite trick of "spa cuisine" chefs—blending ricotta cheese to make a creamy *fromage blanc* with the consistency of very thick cream.

Serves 4

> 1 cup part-skim ricotta cheese
> 2 tablespoons plain low-fat or nonfat yogurt
> 1 teaspoon grated lemon zest
> 2 tablespoons fresh dill, tarragon, or fennel tops,
>   chopped OR ½ teaspoon dried dill
>   or tarragon, crumbled
> 12 ounces tiny cooked and peeled shrimp
> Kosher salt and pepper to taste
> Dash of hot pepper sauce (optional)
> 4 kaiser rolls or other soft sandwich rolls
> ½ cup shredded lettuce

Combine the ricotta, yogurt, and lemon zest in a food processor or blender and blend for a full minute, or until quite smooth. Add the herbs and blend until the herbs are chopped finely. Transfer to a bowl and stir in the shrimp. Season to taste with salt, pepper, and hot sauce. Serve on kaiser rolls, topped with shredded lettuce.

Poached Halibut
with Shrimp Sauce

Thick, crosscut halibut steaks are a common year-round item in fish markets, but they are often cut too large for single servings. Here is a method for turning two large "T-bone" halibut steaks into four servings. The skin and bones from the steaks go into a stock which is both the poaching liquid and the base of the creamy sauce. Of course, if you have a good fish stock on hand, you can use it instead and save the halibut bones for the next batch. Just add the shrimp shells to your stock and simmer for 15 to 30 minutes before straining it over the fish.

Serves 4

> *2 large halibut steaks (8 to 10 ounces each)*
> *⅓ pound small shrimp or rock shrimp meat*
> *4 large green onions*
> *3 sprigs parsley*
> *½ cup dry white wine*
> *3 cups water (approximately)*
> *2 tablespoons unsalted butter*
> *2 cloves garlic, minced*
> *⅛ teaspoon paprika*
> *Pinch of cayenne pepper*
> *½ cup whipping cream*
> *Kosher salt and white or cayenne pepper to taste*

1. Bone and skin the halibut steaks and peel and devein the shrimp. Thinly slice the white parts of the green onions and set aside; cut the green tops into 1-inch pieces. Combine the halibut bones and skin, shrimp shells, green onion tops, and parsley in a saucepan. Add the wine and water to cover. Bring to a boil, reduce to a simmer, and cook 30 minutes, skimming off any foam that rises to the surface. Keep at a simmer.

2. Melt the butter in a skillet over medium heat. Add the garlic, reserved green onions, paprika, and cayenne pepper and cook until the onions soften. Add the shrimp and cook until they turn opaque. Meanwhile, arrange the halibut pieces in a lightly oiled deep skillet just large enough to hold them in one layer. Strain the hot stock over the fish, adding boiling water if necessary to cover the fish with liquid. Bring to a simmer over low heat; do not boil. Poach the fish until done by the skewer test (see Technique Note), about 7 minutes for ¾-inch steaks. If the shrimp get done before the halibut, remove them from the heat.

3. Remove the poached halibut pieces with a slotted spatula, drain them thoroughly, and place them on a warm platter or individual plates. Remove the cooked shrimp with a slotted spoon and arrange them on top of the halibut. Keep warm in a low oven.

4. Bring the poaching liquid to a rolling boil in the poaching pan and boil until flecks of albumin (like egg whites) congeal on top. Strain through a fine sieve to remove the albumin, and add 1 cup of the strained liquid to the shrimp skillet. Bring to a boil, reduce by half, stir in the cream, and reduce by half again. While the sauce is reducing, carefully pour the juices that have accumulated on the halibut platter back into the sauce and blot away any remaining liquid with a paper towel (so it doesn't water down the sauce). Season the sauce to taste and pour it over the halibut and shrimp. Surround the fish with a colorful assortment of julienned vegetables.

Technique Note You can use a small skewer or toothpick to check the doneness of fish without cutting it open. First pierce the raw fish to feel the resistance as the point of the skewer cuts through the muscle fibers. Thoroughly done fish gives almost no resistance. To prevent fish from overcooking and becoming dry, remove it when the very center still offers a little resistance. The fish will continue cooking from the heat on the surface.

Beer Batter Fried Shrimp

East or West, crisp deep-fried butterfly shrimp are so popular in restaurants that I suspect many patrons never order shrimp any other way. Here is my favorite batter for all kinds of fried seafood. The beer gives it both lightness and flavor. Try these shrimp with a simple squeeze of lemon, any of the dipping sauces on pages 111–112, Rémoulade Sauce I (see page 110), or tartar sauce.

Serves 4

> Oil for deep-frying (at least 4 cups)
> 1 pound small or medium shrimp, butterflied
> Flour for dipping
>
> **BEER BATTER**
> 1 large egg yolk, beaten
> ½ cup beer
> ½ teaspoon kosher salt
> ½ cup all-purpose flour

1. To make the batter, combine the egg yolk, beer, and salt in a bowl and stir to dissolve the salt. Gradually add the flour and stir with a whisk until smooth. Cover and refrigerate for at least 30 minutes.

2. Heat the oil in a deep frying pan or wok to 350°. Rinse the shrimp and pat them dry. Holding a shrimp by the tail shell, dredge it in flour, shake off the excess, and dip it in the batter, then slide it carefully into the oil. Cook 4 or 5 at a time until golden brown, 2 to 3 minutes. Adjust the heat so the oil maintains a steady temperature. Drain the cooked shrimp well over the oil, then on paper towels. Transfer to a low oven to keep warm while later batches cook.

Mariko's Teppan Yaki

Teppan yaki is a cooking method rather than a particular dish. It is the kind of tabletop or tableside cooking practiced at some Japanese restaurants, usually with a lot of fanfare and flashing knives. When you dispense with the theatrics, the principle is simple—an assortment of meats, shrimp, and vegetables cooked quickly on a hot surface and served immediately. My wife learned this version from her Japanese roommate Mariko Fujiwara when they shared an apartment in Berkeley, California. She has been serving it ever since.

Serves 4

> 1 whole chicken breast (about 1 pound),
>   skinned and boned
> 2 tablespoons soy sauce
> 2 tablespoons saké
> 1 teaspoon unseasoned rice vinegar
> ¼ pound tender boneless beef (sirloin
>   or tenderloin)
> ½ pound medium or large shrimp, peeled,
>   deveined, and salt-leached (see page 16)
> An assortment of seasonal vegetables, such as:
>   sweet onion, sliced
>   green onions, cut in 1-inch lengths
>   red or green bell pepper, sliced crosswise
>   and seeded
>   fresh asparagus spears, cut diagonally into
>   2-inch lengths
>   1 small Jewel or Garnet yam, sliced ⅛ inch thick
>   large mushrooms, sliced ⅛ inch thick
>   carrots, in thin diagonal slices
> 1 large daikon (Japanese giant radish)
> Cooked rice
> A small pitcher of cooking oil
> 1 lemon, cut into wedges
> Soy sauce for dipping

1. Separate the two muscles of the chicken breast halves. Cut the smaller muscles lengthwise into $\frac{1}{2} \times 2$-inch strips; cut the larger muscles crosswise into strips $\frac{1}{4}$ inch thick. Combine in a small bowl with the soy sauce, saké, and vinegar and marinate 30 minutes.

2. Slice the beef thinly across the grain. (Partially freezing the meat, or partially thawing frozen meat, makes it easier to slice thinly.) Arrange the beef slices and shrimp attractively on a platter with the bowl of chicken in the center. Arrange the sliced vegetables on a second platter. Grate the daikon on the medium or fine side of a box grater (it should come off the grater in fine shreds, not reduced to a pulp).

3. Set each place with chopsticks, a small bowl containing about $\frac{1}{2}$ cup of grated daikon with its liquid, and another small bowl of rice. Place an electric skillet on the table within reach of all the diners; heat to medium low and add enough oil to coat the bottom.

4. Have everyone join in the cooking, placing raw foods in the skillet, turning them, and retrieving them when done, fondue style. While the first round is cooking, each diner can season his daikon to taste with soy sauce and lemon juice. (About 1 teaspoon soy and $\frac{1}{8}$ of a lemon is right for my taste.) Dip the cooked foods in the daikon mixture, then transfer them to your rice bowl to drain for a few seconds. Continue adding foods as space is available in the skillet. Regulate the heat so the food cooks quickly but does not scorch and add more oil as needed. Eat the rice as you go along or save it for the end, when it has soaked up flavor from all the different foods.

Note Use whatever vegetables are in season. I like to include some sort of sweet onion, which may be Texas Granex, Maui, Walla Walla, or Vidalia, depending on the time of year. In summer, try various summer squashes or very thin green beans. Eggplant is not especially suitable, as it tends to drink up all the oil in the pan. In fall, try peeled slices of the more tender varieties of winter squash. Reconstituted dried *shiitake* mushrooms, or fresh if you like them (I don't), could take the place of ordinary mushrooms.

Shrimp Scampi-Style

Scampi is the Italian name for small lobster-like creatures (*Nephrops norvegicus*) also known as lobsterettes, langostinos, or Dublin Bay prawns. In both Italy and America, true scampi are rather rare. The name has come to mean a dish of large shrimp cooked according to the traditional method for scampi, that is, sautéed with plenty of garlic and parsley. In a true Italian meal, scampi would be served all by itself, but feel free to add a rice pilaf and a simple steamed vegetable to the plate.

Serves 4

> 1 tablespoon olive oil, plus more if needed
> 1 to 1½ pounds large or jumbo shrimp, peeled
>   and deveined with tail shells left on
> 2 large cloves garlic, minced
> 1 tablespoon minced shallots
> 2 tablespoons brandy
> 2 teaspoons lemon juice
> 1½ tablespoons chopped Italian parsley
> ⅛ teaspoon kosher salt
> ¼ teaspoon freshly ground black pepper or to taste
> 4 tablespoons unsalted butter, softened

1. In a large skillet or wok, heat 1 tablespoon of the oil to near smoking. (It will get noticeably thinner and slide around the pan as if it were water.) Add the shrimp and cook until just opaque in the center; remove to a warm plate.

2. Add a little more oil to the pan if necessary and add the garlic and shallots. Cook just until fragrant but not browned, about 10 seconds, then add the brandy, lemon juice, parsley, salt, and pepper. Cook until well reduced, then remove the pan from the heat and swirl in the butter. Correct the seasoning.

3. Return the shrimp to the pan and toss them to coat with the sauce, then arrange them on individual plates, tails pointing outward. Spoon the sauce over.

Shrimp Broiled in Butter

Although the whole fennel seeds that season this dish are typical of southern Italy, the technique comes from Louisiana. There, for some inexplicable reason, these shrimp would be called "barbecued," as are any shrimp cooked with a lot of butter and pepper, whether or not they are done on a charcoal grill. Although you can eat this dish with a knife and fork, it's more appropriate to roll up your sleeves and dig in with your fingers, with plenty of napkins on hand. Try it with any good-sized shrimp, especially fresh white or pink Gulf shrimp.

Serves 3 to 4

> 6 tablespoons unsalted butter
> 1 tablespoon whole fennel seeds
> ¼ teaspoon freshly ground black pepper
> ½ teaspoon kosher salt
> 2 tablespoons lemon juice
> 1 pound medium or large shrimp,
>   deveined through the shell
> French bread or cooked rice (optional)

1. Melt the butter in a heavy skillet (preferably cast iron) over medium heat. Add the fennel, pepper, salt, and lemon juice and simmer 5 minutes. Remove from the heat and set aside 15 to 30 minutes for the flavors to mingle.

2. Reheat the skillet over medium-high heat until the butter is quite bubbly. Add the shrimp and cook, turning once, until the shells turn pink. Place the pan under the broiler and cook 4 to 5 minutes. Transfer the shrimp to a shallow serving dish or individual dishes and pour the sauce over all. Peel the shrimp and dip them in the sauce, allowing some of the fennel seeds to cling to the shrimp. If your conscience will allow it, use French bread to sop up the extra sauce, or spoon the sauce over rice.

Shrimp and Corn Pot Pies

Shrimp, corn, and red peppers make a colorful and flavorful filling for a savory pie. Any unsweetened pie dough will do for the topping, but I like to use a tender biscuit dough, as in a fruit cobbler. The key is to avoid overworking the dough. Any excess kneading, or trying to work every last bit of flour into the dough, or even rolling with a rolling pin instead of pushing the dough out by hand will develop the gluten in the flour and result in a tough crust.

Makes 4 single-serving pies

> 4 teaspoons unsalted butter or margarine,
>   plus 2 tablespoons melted
> 1 cup diced red bell pepper (1 medium pepper)
> 1 cup diced yellow onion
> 4 green onions, sliced
> 1⅓ cups corn kernels, fresh or thawed
> ⅛ teaspoon cayenne pepper
> ¾ pound large shrimp, peeled and deveined, diced
> 3 tablespoons flour
> 1 cup unsalted chicken stock
> Kosher salt to taste

> **BISCUIT TOPPING**
> 1⅔ cups all-purpose flour
> 2½ teaspoons baking powder
> ¾ teaspoon kosher salt
> Scant cup whipping cream

1. Prepare the biscuit topping as follows: Combine the dry ingredients in a large mixing bowl and mix thoroughly. Stir in the cream with a fork, stirring just until the mixture is evenly moistened. Turn the mixture by hand in the bowl until most of the floury bits are absorbed. Cover the dough and let it rest for at least 15 minutes.

2. Melt the 4 teaspoons of butter in a saucepan over medium heat. Add the vegetables and cayenne pepper and cook until the onions and peppers soften; do not brown. Add the shrimp and cook just until it begins to turn pink. Stir in the flour and cook 1 minute. Stir in the stock and cook until well thickened. Taste for seasoning and add salt if necessary. Spoon the shrimp mixture into 4 individual bake-and-serve casseroles and set aside to cool.

3. Preheat the oven to 350°. Turn the dough out onto a lightly floured board and press it with fingertips and the heels of your hands to between ⅛ and ¼ inch thick. Cut the dough in quarters and thin out the pieces a little more with your fingertips, if necessary to fit the casseroles. Top each casserole with dough, pressing it against the edges to seal and trimming the excess with your hands. Brush the tops with the melted butter and cut 3 or 4 small vents in the top of each pie. Bake until the crusts are golden brown, about 20 minutes. Serve hot or warm.

Variation To prepare with precooked shrimp, add the shrimp at the end of step 2 after thickening the stock.

Budín de Mariscos
(Tortilla Casserole with Mixed Shellfish)

This rich, lasagne-like casserole is based on the chicken, seafood, and vegetable *budíns* popular in Mexico. A 6-cup soufflé dish just happens to match the diameter of typical corn tortillas, making it very convenient for this dish. You can use raw scallops (whole if small, sliced if large) in the stuffing in place of some of the crab or shrimp.

Serves 4

> *1 can (13 ounces) tomatillos, drained (see Note)*
> *4 green onions, sliced*
> *2 cloves garlic, peeled*
> *3 small green chiles, seeds and ribs removed*
> *¼ cup cilantro leaves*
> *2 tablespoons oil*
> *½ cup unsalted chicken stock*
> *Kosher salt to taste*
> *⅓ pound (scant cup) small cooked and*
>   *peeled shrimp*
> *⅓ pound (scant cup) cooked crabmeat*
> *1 cup sour cream (regular or reduced fat)*
> *½ cup milk*
> *7 6-inch corn tortillas*
> *½ cup grated jack, swiss, muenster,*
>   *or other mild white cheese*

1. Combine the tomatillos, green onions, garlic, chiles, and cilantro in a food processor or blender and blend briefly, stopping before the mixture is completely puréed. Heat the oil in a deep skillet and add the tomatillo purée (carefully—it may spatter in the hot oil). Cook 2 minutes, add the chicken stock, cover, and cook until slightly thickened, about 5 minutes. Add salt to taste and keep warm.

2. Combine the shrimp and crabmeat and moisten them with a little of the sauce. Combine the sour cream and milk in a bowl or measuring pitcher and stir to a smooth, pourable consistency.

3. Preheat the oven to 450°. Place a tortilla in the bottom of a 6-cup round baking dish. Spread a quarter of the tomatillo sauce over the tortilla, top with another tortilla, scatter a third of the shellfish mixture over the second tortilla, and pour a quarter of the cream over all. Repeat twice, making 6 tortilla layers and 3 shellfish layers in all. Top with one more tortilla, then the remaining sauce and cream. Finish with the cheese. Bake 15 minutes or until the top is well browned. Serve hot or warm.

Note Tomatillos are not tomatoes, as the name might suggest, but a similar-looking fruit also known as ground cherries. Look for them in Mexican markets in cans labeled *tomatillo entero*, sometimes with the confusing translation "peeled green tomatoes." If you can find fresh tomatillos (which are becoming more widely available), remove the papery husks and simmer them in water until they get soft and begin to burst, then drain and proceed as for canned.

Garidópita
(Shrimp and Chard Baked in Filo)

I love to match the sweetness of shrimp with tangy, salty ingredients. Feta, the brine-cured sheep's milk cheese of the eastern Mediterranean region, is a perfect example. This dish is a fanciful variation on the Greek *spanakópita*, a savory pie of spinach and feta baked in flaky dough.

Serves 4

> *¾ pound swiss chard*
> *1 tablespoon olive oil*
> *1 small onion, thinly sliced*
> *1 clove garlic, minced*
> *2 teaspoons fresh marjoram, chopped*
> *   OR ½ teaspoon dried oregano, crumbled*
> *¾ pound medium or large shrimp, peeled*
> *   and deveined*
> *2 whole cloves garlic*
> *⅛ teaspoon kosher salt*
> *12 sheets filo (see Note)*
> *4 tablespoons melted butter*
> *⅓ pound feta cheese, well drained and crumbled*
> *   (see Note)*
> *Black pepper to taste*

1. Remove the thick stems from the chard and steam the leaves until the stem ends are tender, about 5 minutes. Remove and rinse with cold water to stop the cooking. Chop finely and drain thoroughly.

2. Heat the oil in a skillet and cook the onion and minced garlic slowly until soft. Add the chard and marjoram and cook until the mixture is nearly dry. Return it to the colander to drain away any remaining liquid.

3. Butterfly the shrimp and smack them once or twice with the side of a broad-bladed knife to flatten them. Pound the whole garlic cloves and salt together to a paste in a mortar, or smash the garlic against a cutting board with the side of the knife, sprinkle it with the salt, and rub the mixture with the side of the knife until it is reduced to a paste. Spread the garlic paste over the shrimp and let it stand 15 minutes. Rinse, drain well, and pat dry.

4. Preheat the oven to 350°. Lay out a sheet of filo dough on a table and brush it lightly all over with melted butter. (Keep the remaining sheets covered with a damp towel to prevent them from drying out.) Lay another sheet of filo on top of the first and brush again. Top with a third sheet. Spoon a quarter of the chard mixture onto the filo, centered 6 inches in from one end; spread it into a 4-inch square. Top with a quarter of the feta and a generous grinding of pepper. Arrange a quarter of the shrimp flat on top of the cheese. Fold the sides of the dough over the filling, then the short end, then roll the package up in the remaining dough, ending up with the shrimp on top and the seam on the bottom. Repeat with the remaining portions.

5. Place the filo packages on an ungreased baking sheet, brush the tops with melted butter, and bake until golden brown and puffy, about 20 minutes. Let cool slightly before serving.

Note Excellent sheep's-milk fetas from Bulgaria (a personal favorite), Greece, Romania, or Corsica are sold in well-stocked delicatessens and cheese shops. Danish and domestic fetas are made from cow's milk and are relatively bland. Feta should be stored in the brine in which it was shipped until the time of sale and used within a week after purchase.

Filo (also spelled phyllo or fillo), or strudel leaves, are paper-thin sheets of pastry sold in one-pound packages in Greek and Middle Eastern delicatessens. Frozen filo is widely available in supermarkets.

Shrimp Creole

Shrimp in a spicy tomato sauce is popular all over the Southeast, but is especially associated with Louisiana. In the summer when fresh, locally grown, fully ripe tomatoes are available, by all means use them for this and other tomato-based dishes; the rest of the year, you are better off using good canned tomatoes.

Serves 4

> *1 pound ripe tomatoes*
> *   OR 1 can (16 ounces) peeled tomatoes*
> *¾ teaspoon kosher salt*
> *1 teaspoon paprika*
> *¼ teaspoon each black and white pepper*
> *⅛ teaspoon cayenne pepper*
> *2 tablespoons unsalted butter or olive oil*
> *   or a combination*
> *1 cup finely diced onion*
> *½ cup finely diced celery*
> *2 cloves garlic, minced*
> *1 large green or red bell pepper, finely diced*
> *Small herb bouquet of thyme, marjoram, parsley,*
> *   and bay leaf (tied with string or in cheesecloth)*
> *1 to 1½ pounds shrimp (any size), peeled*
> *   and deveined*
> *Hot pepper sauce to taste (optional)*

1. Peel the tomatoes, cut them in half, and squeeze out the seeds into a strainer, catching the juice in a bowl. Discard the seeds and chop the tomatoes. (If using canned tomatoes, just halve, seed, and chop them.) Combine the salt, paprika, and peppers in a small bowl and set aside. Heat the butter in a large saucepan and sauté the onion, celery, garlic, and bell pepper over medium heat until they soften. Add the spice mixture and cook another minute, then add the tomatoes with their juice and the herb bouquet. Simmer until the mixture is slightly reduced, about 10 minutes. Remove the herb bouquet. (The sauce may be made to this point a day ahead and refrigerated.)

2. Return the sauce to the heat if made ahead. Taste for seasoning and adjust if needed. Add the shrimp and cook at a simmer until the shrimp are opaque, 3 to 6 minutes depending on size. Serve with rice (either plain white or a mixture of fragrant brown rice varieties). Pass hot pepper sauce for seasoning at the table, if desired.

Stocks and Sauces

Top left: Fresh Basil Mayonnaise.
Top right: Cocktail Sauce.
Middle: Thai Sweet and Sour Dipping Sauce.
Bottom: Rémoulade Sauce II.

Rémoulade Sauce

Tired of tartar sauce? Use one of the following mayonnaise-based sauces with steamed, grilled, fried, or cold shrimp. They are equally delicious with other seafoods, cold meats, or poached chicken.

Rémoulade Sauce I

Makes ¾ cup

> 2 teaspoons fresh tarragon or chervil leaves
> 1 tablespoon chopped parsley
> 1 teaspoon capers, drained
> 1 anchovy fillet, rinsed and chopped
>   OR ½ teaspoon anchovy paste
> ¾ cup mayonnaise, bottled or homemade
> 1 tablespoon Dijon-style mustard

Chop the herbs, capers, and anchovy fillet (if used) together as finely as possible. Combine all the ingredients in a bowl and stir until well blended. Let stand at least 30 minutes before serving. The sauce will keep up to 2 weeks in the refrigerator.

Rémoulade Sauce II (Creole Style)

Makes 1¼ cups

> ¼ cup finely chopped celery
> ¼ cup finely chopped green onions
> ¼ cup chopped parsley
> 2 tablespoons canned pimiento, drained
> 3 tablespoons Creole or Dijon-style mustard
> 2 tablespoons tarragon vinegar
> 1 tablespoon prepared horseradish
> ½ cup mayonnaise, bottled or homemade
> 1 teaspoon paprika
> ¼ teaspoon cayenne pepper
> Dash of Worcestershire sauce
> ¼ teaspoon kosher salt

Set aside half the chopped celery, green onions, and parsley. Place the rest in a food processor or blender with the pimiento, mustard, vinegar, and horseradish. Blend to a paste, then stir into the mayonnaise along with the reserved greens and the remaining ingredients. Let stand 1 hour before serving, to let the flavors develop. Taste for seasoning before serving and correct if necessary. The sauce will keep up to 2 weeks in the refrigerator.

Cocktail Sauce

This is the all-time favorite sauce for shrimp, as well as for other shellfish. Vary the intensity according to your taste by adding or subtracting horseradish and hot pepper sauce.

Makes 1 scant cup

> ¾ cup bottled chili sauce or catsup
> 2 tablespoons minced celery hearts,
>   including leaves
> 1 tablespoon minced green onion or chives
> 1 tablespoon lemon juice
> ¾ teaspoon prepared horseradish (not creamed)
> 3 dashes liquid hot pepper sauce, or to taste

Combine all the ingredients. Let stand at least 15 minutes for the flavors to combine, then taste for seasoning and correct if necessary. The sauce will keep for a week or more, tightly sealed and refrigerated.

Thai Sweet and Sour Dipping Sauce

This sauce is always a hit with my cooking classes. It's equally at home with steamed shrimp, not to mention grilled, poached, or broiled fish, chicken, or pork.

Makes ¾ cup

> 1 tablespoon peanut oil
> ¼ cup finely chopped shallots
> ¼ cup finely chopped garlic
> 1 tablespoon dried hot pepper flakes
> ¼ cup fish sauce (see Note, right)
> 1 teaspoon brown sugar or Chinese golden sugar
> 1 tablespoon tamarind pulp (see Note, page 84) dissolved in ¼ cup warm water
> 2 green onions, finely chopped
> 1 tablespoon fresh coriander leaves (cilantro), chopped

1. Heat the oil in a small skillet and cook the shallots, garlic, and hot pepper flakes until they begin to brown. Remove from the heat and set aside.

2. Combine the fish sauce and sugar in a small saucepan. Strain the tamarind paste through a fine sieve into the saucepan, pressing the pulp with a spoon to extract all the liquid. Bring to a boil, stirring to dissolve the sugar. When the sauce comes to a boil, remove from the heat and stir in the shallot-garlic mixture and the chopped green onions and coriander. Serve warm or at room temperature.

Nuoc Cham (Vietnamese Dipping Sauce)

Variations on this sauce are made all over Southeast Asia. Every region, indeed every cook, has a favorite balance of hot, salty, sweet, and sour flavors, so feel free to vary the proportions to taste. A much hotter variation follows.

Makes a scant ½ cup

> 2 small red or green chiles, seeds and ribs removed
> 2 tablespoons fish sauce (see Note)
> 1 tablespoon rice vinegar or lime juice
> 2 tablespoons water
> ½ teaspoon sugar
> 1 teaspoon chopped fresh coriander (cilantro)

Combine all the ingredients except the coriander in a blender. Blend with a pulsing action until the chiles are chopped into small pieces, but not until they disappear entirely. Let stand a few minutes before serving. Garnish with chopped coriander.

Variation For a hotter flavor, do not remove the seeds and ribs from the chiles. Add a peeled clove of garlic and increase the sugar to 1 teaspoon.

Note Fish sauce, the basic ingredient, is a brown liquid extract made from salted and fermented anchovies. Known as *nuoc mam* in Vietnam, *nam pla* in Thailand (where most of the supply comes from), and "fish's gravy" in Hong Kong, it is used in Southeast Asia much as soy sauce is used in China and Japan—as a seasoning in cooking and a table condiment. Look for it in tall bottles in Asian markets.

Soy-Ginger Dipping Sauce

This is a basic sauce for dipping grilled or steamed shrimp (or other shellfish, or meats, or chicken, or even grilled tofu). Vary the proportions to suit your taste, or better still, set out the ingredients and let guests assemble their own sauces to taste.

Makes ⅓ cup (4 servings)

1 tablespoon grated ginger, with juice
¼ cup soy sauce
1 tablespoon lemon or lime juice, or to taste
1 teaspoon Chinese or Japanese sesame oil
Pinch of sugar (optional)

Combine all the ingredients, stirring to dissolve the sugar. Transfer to individual small bowls for dipping, distributing the ginger evenly.

Variation For a mellower flavor, use rice vinegar in place of the lemon juice.

Variation For a hotter sauce, add a few drops of liquid hot pepper sauce.

Fresh Basil Mayonnaise

I love the bright green of this sauce against the pink of cooked shrimp; I also love the flavor combination. Simple as this sauce is to make, the technique is crucial. To get a deep green stain throughout the sauce, you must crush the basil to a paste—a knife or a food processor won't do it. If you don't have a mortar and pestle, use the back of a spoon or the end of a long knife handle in a china bowl.

Makes 1 cup

1 small handful fresh basil leaves
Pinch of kosher salt
1 cup mayonnaise

Tear the basil leaves into small pieces and combine them with the salt in a mortar. Pound the mixture, grinding it against the sides until the basil is reduced to a very liquid paste. Stir in a tablespoon or two of mayonnaise, then scrape the mixture into a bowl and combine it with the remaining mayonnaise. Serve immediately or let stand up to 24 hours, refrigerated.

Shrimp Butter

Shrimp shells and especially shrimp heads contain a lot of flavor that normally goes into the trash. Some thrifty cook learned ages ago that you can extract the flavor by slowly simmering the shells in butter. Save shrimp heads and shells in the freezer until you have enough to make a batch of butter, then store the shrimp butter in the freezer and you will have a secret source of shrimp flavor to enrich a seafood sauce, boost the flavor of a soufflé or pasta dish, or give an unexpected touch to sauces for poultry.

Makes 1 scant cup

Shells and heads from 1 to 2 pounds of shrimp
1 cup unsalted butter
Pinch of paprika (optional)

1. Spread the shells and heads on a baking sheet and bake in a 400° oven until they turn red, about 10 minutes. Allow them to cool, then chop them as finely as possible by hand or in a food processor. Place them in the top of a double boiler with the butter and cook over moderate heat until the butter has a

noticeable shrimp flavor, about 30 minutes. Adding a pinch of paprika reinforces the natural pale pink color of the shrimp.

2. Strain the mixture and discard the shells. Chill the butter, discard the water which accumulates on the bottom, and freeze in a tightly covered container until ready to use. Shrimp butter will keep up to 3 months in the freezer.

Quick Shrimp Stock

Dishes cooked with stock, such as gumbo, jambalaya, or risotto, get an extra flavor boost if the stock is also flavored with shrimp. It's the easiest way to use those shrimp shells I am always telling people to save in the freezer. The proportions are not critical; use whatever you have on hand. The shells from a pound of shrimp (about 1½ cups) can flavor anywhere from 2 to 4 cups of stock. Baking the shells intensifies their flavor.

Shrimp shells, heads, and broken pieces
Unsalted chicken stock, preferably homemade
OR canned chicken stock diluted with
an equal amount of water

1. (Optional) Spread the shrimp shells on a baking sheet and cook in a 350° oven until bright pink and crisp, about 8 minutes.

2. Chop the shrimp shells as finely as possible with a knife or in a food processor. (Adding a little of the stock may help keep things moving in the machine.) Combine with the chicken stock in a saucepan or stockpot and simmer 30 minutes. Strain through a fine sieve. The stock will be somewhat cloudy; if a clear stock is desired, let it settle for 30 minutes or so and pour the clear stock off the sediment in the bottom, or strain it again through a coffee filter. Use immediately or refrigerate for up to 2 days.

Chicken Stock

Unsalted chicken stock is so basic an ingredient in my recipes that it deserves a place even in a book devoted to shrimp. Canned stock is convenient but often too salty, especially when other salty ingredients are used. There are some unsalted varieties, sold mainly in health-food stores, but none of them can compare with a good homemade stock. Buying whole chickens and cutting them up yourself is by far the most economical way to buy chicken, and it gives you backs, necks, wing tips, and other trimmings with which you can make stock for a few pennies per cup. Save the spare parts in the freezer until you have enough to make a batch of stock.

Makes about 2 quarts

> *2 to 4 pounds chicken parts—backs, necks, wings,*
> *giblets (but not livers), heads, feet*
> *Water to cover*
> *1 large onion, peeled and sliced OR a large handful*
> *of leek or green onion tops*
> *1 carrot, sliced*
> *1 stalk celery, sliced*
> *3 to 4 sprigs of parsley*
> *1 bay leaf*
> *1 sprig of thyme (optional)*
> *1 teaspoon peppercorns*

Rinse the chicken parts well under cold water. If using backs, remove and discard the kidneys, the soft pink masses along the backbone near the tail. Place the parts in a large pot with cold water to cover. Bring just to a boil and reduce to a simmer. Cook 10 minutes, skimming off the foam from the surface. Add the remaining ingredients and simmer uncovered for 1 to 3 hours. Do not let the stock boil or it will become cloudy. Strain the finished stock and refrigerate until the fat solidifies on top; discard the fat or reserve it for another use. If you need to use the stock immediately, skim the fat off with a ladle. Stock will keep in the refrigerator for a week or more if brought to a boil for 5 minutes every third day. Freeze for longer storage.

Index

Italic page numbers indicate photographs.